reflections

Life Reloaded. Class of '87, IIMA

reflections

Life Reloaded. Class of '87, IIMA

'Real-Life Impact Stories' curated by
SANJEEV KOTNALA

Penman Books

Office No. 303, Kumar House Building,
D Block, Central Market, Opp PVR Cinema,
Prashant Vihar, Delhi 110085, India

Website: www.penmanbooks.com
Email: publish@penmanbooks.com

First Published by Penman Books 2019
Copyright © Sanjeev Kotnala
All Rights Reserved.

Title: Reflections: Life Reloaded. Class of '87, IIMA
Price: ₹335 | $ 8.5
ISBN: 978-93-89024-64-7

Dedicated to

The Class of '87, IIM Ahmedabad

Foreword
By Prakash Iyer

School and College Reunions are special. Very special. It's so much fun catching up with old friends, exchanging stories, and talking about individual journeys and experiences. Just the thought that the whole group started off from the same place all those years ago – and has now sailed away in different directions – adds to the variety and the fun. And like someone said, reunions are the only time when you see people not as they are – but as they were!

Sanjeev's book 'Reflections' is a reunion of sorts – with two key differences. The first and more obvious one is that it is a virtual reunion – as batchmates from IIMA's class of 1987 come together in the pages of a book to share their stories and experiences. And the second difference is that this is a reunion where you and I get to eavesdrop and listen in to the stories of mistakes made, battles won and lessons learned.

As someone from the batch of 1986, I often get asked 'Oh, Raghuram Rajan's batch? And I say, no, I was a year senior. In a country where seniority is still a thing, I can almost see the pride in the questioner's eyes at seeing someone 'one year senior to Raghuram Rajan.' Maybe I missed a trick. Should have used that as a headline in my CV! Jokes apart, having spent a year with this batch at IIMA, I could be accused of bias when I state that the batch of 1987 was arguably IIMA's GOAT batch – the Greatest of All Time. It's probably thrown up more young CEOs than any batch before it. Or since. Add the fact that it even has a former Governor of the Reserve Bank to call its own, and you can see why the idea of a book with their reminiscences is such a powerful idea.

As you might expect, there are stories here of doing business around the world, cross-border M&As and jet-setting global bankers. But for me what stands out more are the tales of mistakes made, early-career missteps and lessons learned. It is interesting that most stories go back to the early years, straight out of B School. A time when the comforts of a classroom make way for the dirt and grime of the real world. The fact that successful folks are able to share stories of their mistakes and failures makes this book a nice little read.

There's a lesson from a young kid who avoided getting run out in a game of cricket and learnt a life lesson on never giving up. Stories of life in Mumbai from the lens of someone who couldn't speak a word of Hindi. And this priceless little gem: When asked what do you do, one of the folks from the class of '87 responded "I attend the weddings of the sons and daughters of my batchmates.' When you learn to see life for what it is and learn to live on your own terms, you know you've lived a good life. And the IIMA education has been effective after all.

Knowing several people from the batch of '87. I can say there are many, many more stories waiting to be told. Hopefully, this book will inspire other people from the batch of '87 – and perhaps other batches too – to put together their stories. The world needs to hear those stories. A sequel is surely in the works!

Somewhere in the book is a piece of advice I found interesting: Get yourself an advisory board! You could say that's easier said than done. Ok, do the second best thing then. Read the stories of those folks who could have been on your advisory board.

Prakash Iyer
Leadership Trainer, Motivational Speaker,
Best Selling Author, Former CEO.
and Class of '86, IIM Ahmedabad

"…*each of you is the crème de la crème where you come from. All 180 of you are among the absolutely top percentile talent of the nation. You have topped brilliantly right through your academic term and breezed through the CAT and the tough interview process. You are undoubtedly the very best.*"

"*Now I want you to get ready for a surprise that may hit you if you are not prepared. Your performance here will be graded, and someone will come tops while someone inevitably will be ranked 180th, the bottomer of the class! And half of you toppers will suddenly see yourself in the bottom 50 percentile half of the class, down from the 99 you are used to! A few of you would see yourselves inched out of the race for the gold medal by the proverbial line of split hair. So, be ready for this and don't let it be a nasty surprise anymore. Do not see your middling rank as a failure*".

Prof N. R Seth, Director IIMA,
Addressing the Class of '87,
when they joined the institute in 1985.

A few members of the said Class of 1987, IIM Ahmedabad, contribute the reminiscences appearing here. At no stage should it be Inferred as to include the entire said batch or the institute. No claim express or implied is made that this represents the views / experiences / learning or narrative of those who have not contributed to this compendium. Any reference to any character living or dead, which may be construed as defamatory, is unintentional.

भारतीय प्रबंध संस्थान अहमदाबाद वस्त्रपुर, अहमदाबाद 380 015
INDIAN INSTITUTE OF MANAGEMENT AHMEDABAD Vastrapur, Ahmedabad 380 015
Phone: (D) 91-79-6632 4848 • **Fax:** 91-79-2630 8345 • **Email:** director@iima.ac.in

Errol D'Souza
Director

Another batch from IIM Ahmedabad – the Class of 1987 – and their repertoire of unique experiences shared in this book will resonate within each of us as they depict the many hues of life.

There is the story of the person who after a chance meeting, on an instinct, boarded a plane to far away Sao Paulo. There he gets introduced to guarana, that mood boosting caffeine drink that is oh so Brazil, and business customers who unexpectedly write off short term losses to save a supplier from going bankrupt. Maybe this has to do with the relaxing Caipirinha that he is introduced to and that contributes to the rhythm of life in Brazil.

Another chronicle is that of a consultant who is sent in to by a leading conglomerate to close a subsidiary opened as a start up to provide web services. He finds large orders placed for unused computers and software but is nudged to complete closure of the organization and ignore the assets that were not deployed. Years later at a party at an appropriately high floor in a high-rise he is informed by a suitably spirited person that the conglomerate had appropriated land which it deployed in ways that improved its returns and web services were a ploy for the land deals. Life is clearly not what it appears to be.

Yet another account is of a doctoral student who goes to talk about his proposed topic of research with his advisor but is summarily dismissed and told that unless it is written it is nothing but cheap talk. In the process of writing he begins to understand how the flaws surface in an argument and clarity can be better achieved. This becomes a mantra for living with him so much so that even in disputes with his wife he finds that rather than getting into an argument it is better to jot down and convey what he finds resentful rather than to blow hot. The pen is mightier than the tongue.

There are many other charming stories of how a Group Leader in an organization got a client to make payments by talking about everything but payments and then tangentially bringing it in and obtaining the approval for it without exposing them to loss of face. Or of the promoter from a highly profitable venture who seemed so efficient that it was presumed that he must be highly qualified academically. In fact he just had inherent business capabilities and no qualifications. Some lives are so perceptive that an exposure to formal training and skills is a sheer waste of their time.

I am sure many will be enriched by the narratives in this book. The red bricks of the campus at IIMA have brought stories from different corners and told them in a humane and compelling manner. It is difficult to put away and since it provides so much to reflect on it stays with you even after you have finished reading it.

Errol D'Souza

Reflections
Share The Advantage

Stories are as old as the universe. Millions of stories take birth every moment. Millions of stories reach their end. And, we are part of myriad such stories every moment. We wear masks while performing our duties and responsibilities. We feature as actor, writer, director, instigators, and even observer.

Conceptualizing and finally completing this book is a story in itself. The idea was floated some two years back but not much happened of it. I also parked it aside and got busy in my life.

However, when my second book, LIFE RELOADED, got decent enough appreciation and trended as Number one in Amazon Self-help books for some time, I realized that sharing personal impact stories – *aapbeethi*- can have a great impact on people's lives. The project was revived and here we are with the book – 'Reflections, Life Reloaded, Class of '87', IIM Ahmedabad.

Storytelling predates story-writing. Storytelling as a medium to share knowledge and experiences has been there for long. It will continue till the time we keep discovering new facets in life. Science keeps discovering. So long as we humans have emotions, aspirations, dreams and challenges, stories will continue to prosper.

Yes, with time, the format of storytelling has changed or evolved. We are able to capture more information and tend to lose less with time.

Still, nothing beats *Aapbeethi* (self experience) as a learning medium. The more you experience for yourself, better is your understanding. One can't experience the joy of Paradroping from 13500 feet at Pattaya, Thailand without really getting up there and jumping.

However, life is too short to personally accumulate all experiences. And you can't make every jump. One can learn by observing, listening or just reading about the *Jagbeethi* (experience of others). You don't have to really experience everything.

Every story tells us something new. Globally we have well know stories; Aesop's fables, La Fontaine, Jataka tales, Panchtantra, Akbar-Birbal, Tenali Rama, fairy tales with inbuilt knowledge and wisdom. The stories of war, human ingenuity, cleverness, and mythological legends not only capture the culture and life at a particular time, but are also a manual for life and society.

Similarly, reflection as a process of pausing in life and thinking of what happened, taking a point of an unbiased, neutral observer to happenings in and around us, can give us understanding and wisdom. But, it is tough.

Here is a small attempt at sharing some fresh stories. They are real stories from the lives of people like you and me. Nothing fictional about them.

In the book, 'REFLECTION, Life Reloaded', 18 authors from the IIM Ahmedabad batch of 1987, have boldly and transparently shared more than twenty-five experiences from their professional and personal life. They are small, powerful impact snippets from their life. Incidents that have challenged their thinking or have made an impact on their lives. Read them, just as a small real-life story, or think how would you react, how would you have tackled the situation, responded to the input? Hopefully, a few of them will make sense to you. Who knows what you could gain from these stories?

For ease of reading, the book is divided into five sections. Business, People, Encounter, Life and Institute. Hope you enjoy reading these stories.

Sanjeev Kotnala

Contents

SECTION-D: Life

SECTION-E: INSTITUTE

SECTION-A
Business

Caipirinha Before Wine

A love story of doing business in Brazil

Anchal Jain

It was a particularly pleasant pre-monsoon afternoon in July 1994 when Roy called me and quite uncharacteristically, launched into Hindi. He was inquiring if I could see a couple of young boys from Brazil who just showed up in his trade magazine office. He had no clue what they wanted.

I wondered why he thought I would not only figure out their purpose but also be interested in their visit to India. I was, at that moment, representing a German consortium (Eco-Tex) for ecologically optimised textiles and clothing. I had my hands full with advisory work. Roy dismissed me, saying figuring out things is what IIMA folks are supposed to do.

The young boys from Brazil seemed to be in their early 20s with zero work experience. Probably on a backpacking tour of India, taking a short breather in Delhi before heading off to a Varanasi or a Rishikesh. The shorter and stockier of the two was one talking eagerly in what I could later place as Italian accented Brazilian English.

Frankly, I had no previous knowledge of Brazil, its economy, culture or people. After much effort in trying to understand his animated talk, I figured they were no backpackers. They had made a trip all the way from Sao Paolo to New Delhi in a hope to find some Madras checks fabric. I gave them hot tea and told them they may want to explore Salem, the cotton check town in Tamil Nadu. That's the only word he wrote down in his notebook, "Salem".

Four days later, they were back in my office, this time unannounced.

A month later, in August 1994, I was boarding a plane from New York to Sao Paulo.

I have always been instinctive with my decisions, but this surprised even me. Why would I sign an exclusive agreement to explore business opportunities in a country entirely unknown to me with a twenty-two-year-old stranger who acts like an adolescent? Moreover, a country that is two long haul flights away.

It was an overnighter from New York, but I stayed up reading about what to expect. I knew what caught my attention, it was the boys coming back from Salem. How quickly they had actively seized upon the opportunity that beckoned Brazilian businessmen with just the one thing they knew. The new Finance Minister, Cardoso had announced, a week before their trip to India, the "Real Plan" looking to stabilise the country's inflation woes through the introduction of a new currency to be called "Real", pegged at 1:1 parity with the US Dollar. Significant growth led by consumption was expected, and it would open doors to imports.

I was not much interested in the economic opportunity as the country's music, culture, football and surfing! By the time I landed, I had familiarised myself with some key names. Roberto Gorla, my new partner, was a blonde surfer. The first thing he showed me in Delhi was the picture of his bikini-clad girlfriend, Samantha. At the same time confessing, the only thing he had done before in his life was surfing. It was this very confession that got me to trust his understanding of the surfwear market and its key players in Brazil.

Roberto drove me straight from the airport to his home in Morumbi; a quartier in Sao Paulo. It also houses the final resting place of the legendary Formula One driver, Ayrton Senna. In his pitch inviting me to Brazil, he emphasised on hosting me at his home so that I would have just the flight to pay. This young man had me follow him to the other end of the world after only two hours in my office!

I was completely taken aback by his 'Home'. It had two gardens, a swimming pool, a tennis court, four living suites, two armed guards, and two large German Shepherds. All this for two inhabitants! Samantha welcomed me with a choice between Guarana and Brahma, with Robbie reminding her that the two could also be mixed.

Guarana made me curious. The Guarana seeds contain twice as much caffeine as coffee beans and make a deliciously stimulating, caramel coloured fermented drink. Guarana Antarctica is hugely popular in Brazil and the only soft drink that outsells it, is coca cola. So popular that it sponsors the national pride of Brazil, its football team! I have often wondered why it has not seen success beyond the shores of Brazil.

Thus began my love affair with the country called Brazil and its people.

Robbie left me to relax at the Poolside Suite while he went off to finish the preparations for the big presentation the next day. More than thirty owners of clothing brands were expected at his Mansion to listen to what he had to propose.

My role at the meeting was limited to explaining the rich textile ability India has and all the work I am doing in the domain. As I discovered later, I could well have narrated the story of 'Thursday fasting' of my dear friend and neighbour in Dorm-10 at IIMA, and it would have made no difference. None of them understood or spoke a word of English. Robbie was translating, and I have no idea what narrative he was weaving. I was only there as a living proof that perhaps Indian Textile exists and reassurance that Robbie had a local partner to assure deliveries.

The meeting lasted for over three hours. In the meeting were owners of 22 surf brands, 4 other fashion labels, 1 clearing agent and 2 bankers.

While I understood nothing of the discussion, I could follow the logic of his presentation, the details, planning and research put in by Roberto and his motley team of friends.

The twenty-two-year-old rookie had only one month to put all this together. He went from the economic changes in Brazil to its enormous business implications and other details, arguing for the first-mover advantage. He explained why he picked India and why he picked me. He showcased the fabrics and few finished garments and an idea of landing costs at their warehouse, the likely impact on their profitability, import process, the paperwork involved, payment process and even the negotiated assured limits for a Letter of Credit from the banks.

He ended with a call to action. And then he announced to the bewildered guests that he would take only 15 clients.

In my 32 years of working career, I am yet to meet a better salesman than Roberto Gorla. He had sold his vision of the entire economic value chain by stitching up just two terms that he knew from his practice, "surfing" and "Madras checks". The afternoon taught me the first of my many lessons while doing business in Brazil; real entrepreneurship and the science of selling.

He had his audience in a trance for a full hour and a half before breaking into a discussion. 21 of the 26 businessmen present at the meeting signed up before we ran out of the Caipirinha that evening.

A week later, we were busy making the stay arrangements for the 21 buyers at the fabric and garment manufacturing centres. And we were appointing travel agents at our respective ends to take care of travel to India and within the country.

The events of the two ensuing months are still inexplicable to me.

17 of these 21 owners represented surfwear brands together controlling 95% of the sales in the country. Logistics were a nightmare. We were hosting so many competing buyers each spending a full week in India. To assure timely market deliveries, the schedule had to be fitted within a single buying calendar of a maximum of 5-6 weeks. And then there was the language barrier, which means that Robbie was needed to be in India at the same time he was needed in Sao Paulo.

The solution to the problem was surprisingly simple and human. It was also uniquely Brazilian. 'They are all friends', said Robbie, 'they can embark on buying trips together'.

Surprise, competitors were not only travelling in transparency but also buying in groups of 3 or 4, laying out choices on a common table. Prices were pre-negotiated with the same vendors. Little distinctiveness, no secrecy, all of them enjoying their beer and pizza together at La Piazza in New Delhi while laughing over their respective run-ins during travel.

Alphonse brothers had trouble getting out of a Central London tube station during their long layover, upset that there are no "Exit" signs. Clearly, we had faltered in anticipating the coaching needs for the travelling parties, for in the London tube network, "Exits" are marked as "Way Out".

Robbie's elder sister Gabriella, married to an Italian man with royal ancestry near Rome was tasked with translation. Hence, while the buyers were in India, she found herself on a plane almost every day for five weeks.

Gabriella was ready to murder Robbie and me by the end of the circus. Instead, she settled for selling out her brother's dark secrets to me including the time when their Dad had to call in the police (on his own son) in the dead of night to bring a wild house party to an end. The other stories are better off narrated just orally.

We clocked a few million dollars worth of business from a standing start. It defied logic under any circumstances. I was to learn a few months after the first delivery that each one of the brands reported excellent sales. They had ended up stretching the market for surf shorts 6x in one season.

What gave these 17 men the courage to buy so much of similar product in one category? So what if it was distinctive for their market?

Did they even realise that together their buying would imply that under normal organic growth conditions, they would have all been left holding huge stocks?

Why did the market explode, was it down to just new economic dawn in the nation?

Surely the consumers do not react so swiftly to economic reforms.

I was just beginning to work with Trend Forecast bureaus in France and understood very little of it. None of the creative geniuses in Paris could satisfactorily explain to me how these fashion trends manipulate customers into believing the grand prognosis by the "experts". What gave them the right and the confidence to pronounce what the customers will love eighteen months before anyone would even see them in the market?

I saw the answer play out right in front of my eyes.

The insight I drew from the Brazilian adventure was logical and straightforward, fashion trends are simply an organised supply of goods with at least one common thread. Each one of the 17 had expanded their market while attracting the consumer attention to surf shorts in Madras checks. Their own signature in garment styling was the only distinction.

This learning would serve me immensely in the following decades of my brush with fashion trend forecasting. It was also a lesson in the niche, cult marketing.

Surfwear was for a particular tribe with a specific lifestyle but was now fast becoming the new expression in Street Style. These 17 friends heard out another of their tribe, a customer actually. Together they convinced more of their fellow countrymen.

Over the next two years, I became friends with them but simply couldn't surf, just as I never could learn to do the salsa. But, I learnt a great deal about Carlinhos Brown, Gilberto Gil, Seu Jorge, Joao Gilberto, Jorge Ben Jor and other amazing musicians from the land of Samba, Bossa Nova and the "Carnaval". It was my introduction to Latin music, later extended to Salsa, Afro-Latin Jazz rounded off with touches of Andalusia.

The music continues to be my "safe place" even today.

I learnt even more about Caipirinha. I cannot make up my mind if I love it so much thanks to my love for Brazil or the other way round. Either way, I cannot isolate the three from each other. Add to the mix, I loved listening to the melodious Brazilian Portuguese. Just a "Quem Fala" ("Who's speaking") when answering a phone call sounded like a whole song!

By 1996, Roberto and I had fallen out, although I continue to nurture the most amazing and fascinating memories of our time working together. By now, I had consolidated my base in Paris. It was time to again look at the Brazilian market with a fresh approach and structure.

I couldn't have found a more contrasting partner for Brazil. Edson was a tall, polished professional. A devout church-going

Protestant family man, ten years my elder with two kids in teens.

My earliest memory of Edson is of him hosting me for dinner at his place. Edson is playing every Gilberto Gil song he loves while attempting to translate each line in English. He kept going for almost two hours. I never found the heart or the courage to tell him that even when listening to English or Hindi music, words do not matter to me. Music talks to me in a different language altogether.

With Edson, we opened up an entirely different market segment. The one that I personally and intuitively connected with and where I felt I was in control. The results were stunning. We were soon working with seven of the largest brands in the mainstream mid to premium fashion segment.

The big difference in our approach was that while earlier we were acting as buying agents earning a small commission, now we were invoicing the customers from Paris. It meant more control over the supply chain and significantly more margins. The new customers also spoke English!

I was now discovering the "Churrascaria", despite being a vegetarian. Churrascaria is a Brazilian barbeque restaurant with meat being carved at the table itself. The servers would keep bringing around different parts of the animals, deftly and swiftly carving out whatever a diner wanted.

The experience fascinated me even as I was repelled by the notion. I kept going back, for that is where I found the freshest and most delicious Palm Hearts, Asparagus or Artichokes in an always very generous salad bar. And, on our road trips to clients, Edson and I would stop at the humblest country canteens serving daily lunch Buffets where one pays by the weight loaded on the plate. The simple black beans and rice.

Swinging between the humble and the exotic was like a samba beat from Bahia. Strangely, I never got curious about

Rio de Janeiro or its Copacabana beach. I still don't know why. I think I reject the obviously expected. Perhaps that is why, after spending decades in Paris, I never climbed the Tower Eiffel or saw the inside of the Louvre.

I never felt I was working in Brazil. It was always a pleasant happy trip amongst friends. Going fishing or surfing (well watching them surf) or just playing football with the customers was normal. Yet, they were serious at work, very professional. They were also more sincere and human than any other businessmen, anywhere in the world. This, I was to soon discover.

In January 1999, the day one of my seasonal sales trip to Sao Paulo saw a particularly bumper harvest with two of our biggest buyers. They loved what was presented and made a much more extensive selection. They asked us to come back the next morning to take the order details.

It was an early start the next morning, and we were at the customer's doorstep at 8:30am. A warm welcome later, Claudio pushed the front page of the newspaper towards us. Buckling under the pressure from the Russian financial crisis and the consequent flight of Russian capital from Brazil, the newly elected President had decided to float the Real (R$) on the open market after four years of tight monitoring. Overnight the Real had devalued 80% to almost 1US$: 2R$.

To complete the closure of the markets, the import duty had increased from 20% to 80%.

It was a very short meeting. Claudio showed us the orders, but he couldn't go through with it. He gave me a hug and regretted that the business must come to an end.

Driving back, a bigger and more immediate concern hit me. We had 40 container loads of merchandise on the high seas. We had back-to-back commitments to all our suppliers in India. I would be bankrupt even if a couple of the customers failed to honour the Letter of Credits. And here we have exposure to seven. The goods on landing will be over 2.5 times more expensive than budgeted. My partner in Paris and I were resigned to a total cleanout of our business.

Edson's phone started to ring, and it rang six more times in the day.

Each time, it was one of the customers calling to speak to me. Each one was saying the same thing. They will miss doing business with me. However, they will honour their commitments towards the goods on the sea.

Apparently, it was a collective decision the customers made to show their appreciation and regret. They were willing to write off short term losses to save a supplier from going bankrupt, knowing fully well that they have little use of the supplier in the foreseeable future.

It was difficult to fly back to Paris, bid goodbye to Edson, his family that had adopted me. To the land and people that had given me so much love and joy.

But Brazil kept giving.

As if on cue, just days following my return, I got a call from the Product head at Speedo. He was wondering if I could make a trip to Nottingham to explore a new product category the brand wanted to get into. Surf inspired beachwear.

Half-heartedly and not expecting much from the trip, I drove off with exactly two pairs of shorts in my bag from what we had done for Brazil. I hesitantly laid them out. Chris, the Product Head and his designer kept staring at the two pieces for eternity and looking at each other. Eventually, Chris turned to me and asked if I had anything else to show. I shook my head. Then he spoke slowly, "I cannot believe that the pieces we are looking at are exactly what we had dreamt of. Would you like to work on the entire project with us?"

Thus began a new chapter in "surfing" and "Madras checks" saga. I may have abandoned Brazil, but Brazil never left me. Just four years and I had a lifetime's fill.

Even today, before I order my favourite wine in Paris, I look for Caipirinha as an aperitif. And then remember how Eduardo Rizk had taught me to make it with the right balance of Cachaca, acidity, sweetness and crushed ice. The taste should never dilute until the last sip, he had said. Just like Brazil.

Literacy is But Chickenfeed!

N. Subramaniam

As a Private Equity investor, I was fortunate to have had exposure to a hugely diverse range of businesses. It ranged from sexy internet ventures (DotCom 1.0 in the year 2000) to neat FMCG to foul (pun intended) poultry farming/chicken breeding and mundane milk vending, all the way to marginally branded recycling of PET bottles, a very dirty business indeed.

I once had to convince a poultry farm (Let's call them XYZ Co.) owner in South India about our expertise and the value of associating with us. His business was the largest, the most successful and of course as profitable as can be. I was trying my best to impress upon him something not so complicated. Though money is an unbranded commodity, why the value-added money which comes at the right time, from the right investors can amplify Business Valuations substantially.

It was a very competitive situation. I was pitched against IFC World Bank. A developmental finance institution for whom return metrics were of low priority as compared to employment generation, income distribution, poverty alleviation, etc. There were also a couple of other private Players who had come with financial intentions similar to ours.

XYZ was clearly an amazingly well-run company with great systems and processes in place and was like a Business-Fairy tale. It had been growing at about 15% pa, across economic cycles, for over a decade. It had more than critical mass in terms of size of operations (then about Rs 40 Billion). It had a well-defined organisation structure. It had qualified professionals owning various responsibilities. The company had created a unique business model of having over 5000 farmers running 'conversion farms'. The farmers would be delivered tiny hatchlings. They would also be supported with information and training programs, feedstock, vaccination, debeaking, indeed any software and hardware required to transform a small chick into a well-grown bird for consumption in 6 weeks. In effect, the farmer was an outsourced jobber running a fully supported production unit. I am NOT digressing into an Animal Husbandry lecture. I need you to be familiar with this to convince you about the technical, operational and financial expertise of a firm that is robust enough to run such an extended network like clockwork.

The Profit and Loss Account of the company was known up to the previous day. I saw this every day, over three days that I spent there.

Sales were for cash in the *mandis*. No holidays in the calendar year. There were impressive controls over every matrix. Be it cash handling, unit price realisation or total realisation across the country, the weight of birds sold or cold chain integrity. You name it, and they had mapped it.

It was a dream case in Management Control Sytems.

List all the vectors of this business, how it is run, the Vision and Values of Promoter, in every which way it was the perfect marriage for any Private Equity Investor.

My fund was no exception. We hunted for growth businesses led by Visionary Promoters with high values. XYZ was a dream deal, and we HAD to win this !!

I thought, I definitely had the edge over some of the others. I fluently spoke the language of the promoter. My College and the company headquarter were in the same town. With my networking, there should be some good connections. Homework helped me estimate the age of the promoter and therefore, college cohort and friends. I had already met him informally among his Rotary Club friends, the night before our formal appointment. I had an excellent visual fix of him.

However, the 'connect' was eluding me. No one in the Rotary group knew which College he had gone to. Nothing was helping. My being a College Union Leader (!), extensive participation in Intercollegiate activities including protest strikes (!), Quiz and Debate competitions proved to be of no help.

I estimated that the promoter must be of my age. At best a year or two younger and therefore I even checked with junior cohorts. I was reasonably confident that there was a significant chance of the promoter knowing of me, or finding out about me. I intended to connect to him through some of his batchmates across colleges if I could pin them down. The idea was simple, such connect(s) could help in establishing rapport/camaraderie so that we could meet, discuss and eventually enter into a business partnership comfortably.

But even by the time the actual meeting took place, I had no such information. I was still curious to ascertain the College where the promoter had qualified: graduation, post-graduation, MBA and so on. Over lunch on the second day, I asked him if he went to College in the town where the company operations were headquartered and if so which College?

I was not only shocked but also shamefully silenced by his response "My Anna (elder brother), is a graduate". Clearly, this was not the first time that he was facing such a question about his education, and about his not being a graduate. I had been so carried away by the meticulous and robust Organisation he ran and the power of his vision and ability to execute flawlessly. I firmly believed he must be superbly qualified academically, only to be silenced and humbled by his response!

On that day, I reflected upon the interaction and realised that professionally run companies are not necessarily run by professionally qualified people. Earthy, rustic and intuitive common sense is capable of building sustainable, high growth business. I was convinced of the humility of the promoter and humbled enough to never again be misled about the relationship between qualifications and capabilities.

It is Tough Building an Organisation, but the Lessons Learned are Simple

S Subramanian

Why am I telling this story?

I was bored of working in the steel industry for two decades and was thrilled when an opportunity came to be the first employee and head of Wigget Services (TN), a service organisation. It was something different. The assignment was to set up a state-wide spatially distributed 24 x 7 emergency ambulance service in Tamil Nadu under Public Private Partnership with assets belonging to the government, and the employees on the rolls of Wigget Services (TN). The emergency call number was 108, with any emergency call being responded to by a centralised call centre at Chennai, which would locate the ambulance closest to the medical emergency for evacuation.

While serving my notice period before joining Wigget Services (TN), my thrill turned into despair. I had never handled teams of more than fifteen people and that too within a specific functional specialisation. Now, I was expected to start from scratch, scale it up and operate a service organisation that may have one thousand plus employees.

Fortunately, setting up and running a state-wide Emergency Response Ambulance service in Tamil Nadu for Wigget Services (TN) turned out to be an exhilarating experience. We were getting into an unchartered territory. There was no source for talent with prior managerial experience in the category.

The Story

Cut back to 1st April 2008. I moved to Chennai after spending two months at Wigget Resources (HQ) at Hyderabad, to get the hang of the operations in Andhra Pradesh. Though around three hundred emergency ambulances were operating then in Andhra Pradesh, the launch and growth (which took place in fits and starts) had been over a period of time while the plan for Tamil Nadu was to reach three hundred ambulances in seven months. There was little I could discern of the birth pangs of starting up emergency ambulance service at Hyderabad.

The proposal for an MOU with Tamil Nadu government had been on the anvil for six months when I moved to Chennai. I had no office, and I used to play musical chairs in the PPP cell of Directorate of Medical Services. A verbal commitment to sign the MOU came from the highest level in Tamil Nadu Government in mid-April'2008. This was followed by three tension-filled weeks as there was intense pressure to engage another organisation. Finally, our MOU was signed in mid-May'2008. I was allocated a doorless cubicle with a large centre desk and ten chairs in a large shed in Directorate of Medical Services complex as start-up space. We operated from this cubicle for three months.

On 1st June 2008, I had a three-member team of Angelin, Vanita and Williams. Our only tools of the trade were two laptop computers and our mobile phones. My team members were all half my age!

We advertised vacancies in the local newspaper and employment exchanges. Walk-in interviews for paramedics at Chennai, Madurai and Coimbatore were held simultaneously on 8th June. We got twenty-two candidates. They were all from outside Chennai, from the ninety offers we made. We sent them to Hyderabad (head office) for four weeks of training. There was confusion fuelled by language issue, geographic unfamiliarity and absence of facilitation team at Hyderabad. Hence the next batch from Chennai was directly sent to hostels at Hyderabad.

The second walk-in-interview on 22nd June was held simultaneously at Vellore, Madurai, Chennai and Coimbatore. It gave us forty-four candidates from three hundred offer made. The succeeding Saturday, the successful candidates assembled on arrival at Koyambedu (interstate bus terminal: Chennai) and Egmore railway station, Chennai. They boarded the bus for Hyderabad where they were scheduled for a three week training.

Summer is a rush period for travelling. Hence we had to book bus/train tickets well in advance. After internal discussion and length deliberations, we had reserved eighty seats and thus lost taxpayers money, paid for the unused thirty-six seats.

Our young team of Angeline, Vanita, Williams and not so young Shankar were bewildered at the abysmal ratio of candidates on board to the number of offers made, especially in the second round of recruitment.

After collective deliberation, we attributed some plausible reasons for poor turnouts as

- Wigget Services (TN) was an unknown entity In Tamil Nadu. Such large-scale recruitment for ambulance service was unheard of. It was never done before.
- Just a photo of MOU signing event and newspaper articles saying it was a state government initiative alone

was not enough build up trust overnight. We had no office address in Chennai!

- In that period, there were some major fraud cases like the gold coin scheme, people were uneasy and uncomfortable at being recruited and sent to Hyderabad on short notice.

- Wigget Services was promoted by an Information Technology czar. However, Satyam, Wipro and Infosys, the big names in Information Technology were known only to urban educated people. They meant nothing to the masses at large.

As the first step to increasing awareness and credibility of our organisation, we requested the candidates undergoing training at Hyderabad to speak to their friends and relatives. It had a tremendous effect once we shifted to new premises on the eve of Independence Day. We started getting walk-in candidates.

In fact, walk-in candidates from across the state selected in the last week of August formed the majority of the 370 paramedics we had on board in October 2008.

We realised that everyday walk-in was disturbing our work schedule and other tasks were suffering, so somewhere in October, we consciously moved walk-in to Wednesday. This eased out things a bit.

Learning One: Seeing is believing and there is no better proof for the intention of purpose. Anybody walking into our office would immediately feel that our organisation in our new premises meant business, serious business.

The first two rounds of recruitments for paramedic trainees left us bruised. We had to build self-belief that we could do better. Somewhere, Williams managed to cull out data on initial launches by Wigget Services (GJ) in Gujarat, and we got our breath back. It was not an impossible task. In a lighter vein, I used to tell my team it was my fault- my decision to take up the position on 1st April, April Fools' Day!

After considerable deliberation, we decided that paramedic training at Chennai would attract more candidates. We checked the status of Emergency Medicine Training Team (EMTT) recruitment. We had three doctors and nine EMLC trainers on board for Chennai undergoing induction at Hyderabad.

In the situation we found ourselves in, we did not pay attention to infrastructure availability. We took this decision of having training in Chennai on 30th June. We realised, we needed to inform the recruits of the training venue during the interview.

Learning two: We can plan, plan and plan. However, there are occasions when a quick decision needs to be taken intuitively. Procrastination only delays the process, without any commensurate improvement in the quality of the decision. The sheer pressure of a deadline could enable us to put together resources in time.

We were holed up in our cubicle in the Directorate of Medical Services (DMS) campus from the start. Our administrative set up was already twenty strong on 30th June'2008. We had to zero in and find classroom and hostel facility at short notice.

Through our nodal agency TN Health Systems Project (TNHSP), we located a suitable venue – Institute of Public Health, Poonnamallee (IPH in short - a colonial institution with the tree-lined avenue, duck pond and sylvan surroundings). Fortunately, they did not have an in-house program for a couple of months and this suited us.

Our recruitment drive in four cities across Tamil Nadu on 8th July secured us 65 candidates for training in Chennai- a significant improvement over our first two efforts.

On 13th July, we were told about a host of things required to commence EMLC training for the launch in Tamil Nadu. We, like determined soldiers, swung into action. We caught the trainers coming back from Hyderabad after induction. We asked them to carry some voluminous paraphernalia with them by rail.

Our trainers boarded the train from Hyderabad on 15th July with loads of books, projector, screen etc. They proceeded straight to IPH in time for registration of candidates on 16th July. We made several trips to Poonnammallee (about 30 km from Chennai) putting things in place and sending additional ammunition after the commencement of the course. Our team worked seamlessly. They were oblivious of their positions in the hierarchy of our organisation. It was as if the hierarchy did not exist.

EMLC Trainers group was the first full-grown unit to fall in place in Wigget Services (TN). Some of the trainers merged to create a well-knit group straight away. A few needed coaxing. Couple of them proved to be difficult and had to be hammered into the group! In due course, the team had swelled to fourteen, and subsequently conducted training parallel for several batches with aplomb.

We had plenty of letter writing to do. Everything related to training like hospital rotation phase, external examination formalities, bulk booking in trains for ambulance phase training and other coordination had letter writing. Initially, the core team did the whole thing. Then, we pushed the EMLC training team to take up responsibility and asked them not to worry if they make mistakes during the process. We reassured them that the errors were inevitable in the process of learning and the essence of the learning process was not to repeat the mistakes. We also made it absolutely clear that the trainers and trainees must escalate a situation immediately if they sense smoke as there can't be smoke without fire.

The EMLC team started performing all the functions on their own asking for help/direction only when a new activity/coordination was required.

Lesson three: (a) Mistakes are inevitable in the process of learning. The essence of learning is not to repeat those mistakes (b) if a serious mistake happens despite best effort, keep your superiors informed.

In the meantime, the first batch of twenty-two paramedics trained at Hyderabad returned to Chennai on 21st July. This batch comprised of twelve girls and ten boys. None of them were from Chennai. They were all feeling homesick. We allowed them a break to go home and return the next week.

On return to Chennai, this first batch of paramedics needed a place to stay, and they had to fend for themselves. Angeline and Appadurai ran around trying to fix up accommodation for this trained batch. They visited several hostels. In most places, there was no accommodation available at such short notice. Where it was possible, the advance deposit was a stiff amount. Appadurai felt he had zeroed in on an appropriate hostel facility for men while Angeline had found out a hostel at Adyar for girls.

The twenty-two paramedics reported for work on the following Monday. The girls went along with Angeline and had a look at the hostel. They found it too expensive, and of course, they did not have any money to pay as advance. They were in constant touch with their parents. It became clear to us that if we were unable to solve their accommodation issue, they would go back, leaving us high and dry. The girls were sitting with their luggage in an open space in Directorate of Medical Services complex the whole day and pestered Angeline and Vanita whenever they passed by. I was spared by them, I suspect not because of respect for decision-making capabilities but out of pity for my helplessness!

The boys left in the evening for the accommodation arranged by Appadurai.

In a moment of inspiration, we rang our trainers staying at IPH and asked them to find out whether the hostel was fully occupied. We found out that the hostel could accommodate fifteen more girls. We approached the campus-in-charge. We told her that twelve trainees would be on outdoor training for fifteen days and if they could be given accommodation. To our surprise, she agreed, and finally, all of us heaved a sigh of relief. Williams and I squeezed in these twelve girls in our vehicles and dropped them at IPH. For a long time, the joke among the team was that I was the only state head who had chauffeured girl paramedics!

Trouble continued the next day. The boys had spent the night sleeping at Central Railway station as the hostel arranged by Appadorai was not to their liking. Through Tamil Nadu government officials, we were able to get rooms at Nehru Stadium where athletes were billed for training/ competition at Rs 30 per head per day. The accommodation was provided to our paramedics for just a week. However, our paramedics used their persuasive skills to stay on for three weeks.

All these girls and boys managed to find accommodation on their own with assistance from our team by the time they had to vacate IPH / Nehru Stadium premises.

These girls and boys saw in close quarters the pains we took and vexatious moments we passed through to find them accommodation. They appreciated the efforts and thanked our administrative team profusely.

This action won us their trust. This group of paramedics spread the message to other paramedics who had subsequently joined us. This strengthened the image of Wigget Resources (TN).

Lesson four: In the initial days, parents used to accompany paramedic recruits on the first day they reported to work. They were uncomfortable when they found out that we did not have an office address.

We went to great lengths in explaining how we would look after our associates but there was disquiet among the parents. Trust is the cornerstone around which organisations are built. In this case, concern for Associates. After training, they had landed in Chennai without accommodation. Our administration did everything possible to help them find accommodation, despite ourselves being hamstrung for resources. This is what sparked the building of trust for our organisation.

Then came the turn of hiring drivers for the Ambulances. The process of recruiting them followed a similar trail of paucity, hick-ups, peer recommendations and situation of plenty. The Call centre employee recruitment turned out easier with all recruits hailing from Greater Chennai area. By the time functional heads for human resources, finance and accounts, procurement and call centre got on board, we were three hundred strong. Till this stage, it was a lonely furrow for me as a manager rowing through unchartered territory.

We shifted to our premises and earned our permanent address on the eve of Independence Day. We occupied a standalone two-story building with a quadrangle. It was a sixty-year-old hostel building which we modified extensively to accommodate our office, stores, call centre, training rooms and meeting rooms.

The moment of truth was on 15th September 2008. The ambulance service was launched by Tamil Nadu Chief Minister. There were ten ambulances strategically stationed across

Chennai. The fleet was in position by 12 noon. The emergency number to dial for emergency service was 108. We waited in the call centre for the first emergency call. Several calls frustrated us. Most of them were enquiry calls.

Finally, a passer-by called reporting a road accident at 10.15 pm near Guindy. Our ambulance reached the spot within ten minutes and evacuated the injured. We all cheered when the ambulance driver reported the ambulance was leaving the accident spot on its way to the hospital. And the injured was admitted to hospital casualty ward by 10.50 pm- well within "The Golden Hour". That was some relief and some joy of sheer delivering what we promised.

By March 2009, we had 300 emergency ambulances operating across the state of Tamil Nadu catering to a broad swathe of public. The employee count reached one thousand seven hundred. Currently, Wigget Services (TN) is operating with 936 emergency ambulances in Tamil Nadu.

Does the story end here?

Yes and no. This experience, besides letting me discover different aspects of me as a professional, has turned me into a storyteller! There are always other stories- for another time.

All Races in Africa are not Long

Gyaneshwar Tripathi

"Thank you very much all of you; Trips, any other Business for the Board?"

Chairman's question did not surprise me. It was his formal way of ending every Quarterly Board Meeting of Steel Manufacturing Company LLC (SMCL) (Name changed), and this board meeting had no reason to be different.

He was not very happy, although the Board meeting had gone well and the results were quite good on the back of stable steel prices despite subdued demand.

Our steel plants in the Gulf had performed well during the quarter in question. The delta between reinforced steel bars (rebars) selling prices and steel scrap prices had been maintained and conversion costs were also under control.

Our new steel plant in a neighbouring country was also operational based on power drawn from DG Sets. Although power connection from the state-owned utility would come later, steel melting process had commenced and in-house produced billets were now available to the rolling mill in small quantities. However, the demand for Rebars was still sluggish. Scrap availability at the right price was a challenge, and the customers were pressing for long credit periods, while our policy was to sell only against cash or L/Cs.

The Board was not very happy with the CEO and CFO (me) because of the slow ramp-up of the rolling mill in the neighbouring country as both of us were on the Board of the subsidiary and were running it hands on.

I sought permission of Chairman to table an additional agenda item, "Sir, there is one item I want to table for the Board's consideration. It's about our Africa Steel project and needs to be taken up immediately"

Chairman had an idea about what I was driving at although I had not included it in the formal agenda. While I had circulated a detailed note in advance to the Board members, he had advised me to put up the proposal in the Board meeting for consideration.

The Board members were looking forward to the meeting coming to an end. They expected me to wrap it up but I was about to spoil everyone's lunch.

"Ok Trips, go ahead," said the Chairman.

"Based on Chairman's advice, I travelled last week and conducted a review of our project in Africa. I had circulated my note to the Board at the end of last week and hope that all of you had a chance to look at it. I have copies of the note which I am handing over once again for ready reference". There were four others in the Boardroom apart from Chairman and me, the Senior Most Director (SMD), our Ex-CEO who was an External Director (ED), Director of Group Investments (DGI) and our present CEO.

SMD who sat across me looked anxious. Being a very capable and accomplished professional and with a long stint with our Group, he was optimistic on African Steel as the project feasibility studies had shown high and quick returns. ED who was sitting next to SMD was one of the most competent professionals I have ever come across. He was my guide and being a steel expert he had evaluated the risks independently. He had started the project, we got along well and he was convinced with my view of the increased risks. So he had my back. The DGI was a very competent analyst and was neutral and would handle each issue professionally. CEO was a slightly unhappy as he was personally committed to growth of the company and genuinely wanted to explore all opportunities.

My work was cut out for me. I had to convince SMD and DGI. CEO would express his professional view to all which will help. ED would give his expert opinion which will have lot of weight as always in the Board. Chairman would not reveal his view till the end. So I aimed to have 3 Directors convinced on my recommendation and leave it for Chairman to decide.

"Yes, we have seen the note. So what's the best course of action, Trips" asked SMD.

True to my style, I stated my position instantly and bluntly. "I am recommending that we cease the construction of our steel plant, abandon the project and exit. We can write off our investments and search for a potential buyer. Someone who can buy our assets on the ground and possibly the plant and machinery too which is yet to be shipped to Africa. This is our 2nd project in Africa, and after our earlier bad experience with the failed manufacturing venture, we don't want another failure after we start operating. The business environment has sharply deteriorated, forex availability has dried up and the operating risks are too high; so I recommend that we exit without any delay and cut our losses."

There was a stunned silence in the Boardroom. The Board meeting had just got extended.

The Board room suddenly appeared too cold and we asked the office boy to increase the temperature. I corrected the knot of my tie, a long standing sign of my nervousness.

All Directors got busy reading the executive summary of my detailed note once again. Chairman was his usual relaxed self. He was an eminent citizen of one of the dominant Gulf countries with impeccable character and integrity. Moreover, he was the sole owner of one of the largest and most successful industrial groups and a very competent businessman, so this write-off was not a very big deal for him. Still, it was a big loss and any damage was undesirable for him. However, it was a disappointment for the new CEO who had been backing the project and was keen to implement it as he was committed to company's growth.

After about 30 minutes of discussions on my note and after we successfully answered Chairman's questions and with valuable expert advice from the ED and CEO, the Chairman agreed to my recommendation. We were exiting. He directed us to work on the exit mechanism.

Background; get familiar with it to appreciate what was happening.

The story of our Africa investments was quite old. Our ED who was the founder CEO of SMCL, had worked extremely hard on setting up our Africa projects since 2011. It was in one of the mountainous countries south of Sahara desert. Lets call it AFRICA ONE.

In 2011, we had divested our large steel manufacturing investment in Gulf. These included our prestigeous projects; 3 factories that were set up over a 4 year period with a lot of sweat and grind for Sponge Iron, Billet manufacturing and Rebar Rolling Mill.

In line with the Board & Shareholders' strategy of remodeling the business, ED and I worked on the divestiture transaction. We managed to complete the asset sale at a record valuation to one of the public enterprise in the country.

Taking our divestment strategy further, we had commenced divesting from our power equipment manufacturing as well. The Shareholders too were of the view to exit the relatively complicated manufacturing sector of power equipment and consolidate in the steel and polymer sectors. The first stage of selling the companies based in Gulf countries had been completed, and the divestment of another 100% owned subsidiary was in progress.

All these divestments were considerable achievements by our ED and me. We had managed to do the deals at very attractive valuations under ED's leadership with minimal assistance from external legal and financial advisors. You can say (and I can boast), it was fully due to the efforts of the two of us.

On one side, we had got out of the larger steel plants, on the other hand, we were in the process of setting up smaller steel plants at demand centers. In the process, we were setting up a steel melting and rolling unit in Africa One.

The Learning Happened Fast In Africa

SMCL's Africa strategy was facing continuous hurdles. In our first foray into Africa, we started with a power equipment manufacturing JV (Joint Venture) in a 50% partnership with a local businessman.

The project went into commercial operations in 2014. Within 6 months, we could see that the project was struggling mostly due to issues unrelated to business. It was becoming difficult to work with the local partner, and by 2015 we decided to exit the business by offering to sell our stake to the local partner.

We hired the country's best known law firm of Mohamand & Associates (Name Changed) as our legal advisors. The law firm was associate of one of the top law firms of USA. And the only BIG 4 (name with-held) Accounting firm in the area as our Auditors and Advisors.

The way SMCL operated, financial management was in our hands. However, it was becoming difficult to manage the finances of the African JV. The banks were unwilling to lend to us any working capital till the land was transferred in the company's name. The local partner who had provided the land was creating a problem and was unwilling to transfer the land in the company's name.

Finally, after evaluating our options, we struck a deal with our partner and sold our shareholding at a significant loss. It was not easy to convince the Chairman as ED was not fully convinced for the sell-out at such a loss. He was right in his professional view but I was impatient to get out of the messy partnership. The photo finish to the deal happened just one hour before we had to leave for airport to take the flight back to Dubai.

In a final meeting with the African partner in the lobby of the plush 5-star Hotel, I convinced the Chairman to sign the deal. He signed and we got into the car for the airport. I always enjoyed travelling with Chairman as we both enjoy fine dining, good food and I got upgraded from Business to first class when travelling with him.

The JV fiasco in Africa One taught me two big lessons.

LESSON no. 1: If the law allows for 100% foreign ownership, do not do any partnerships with any local person, unless you are entering a restricted sector. The local partners end up creating more problems than facilitating Government/ statutory approvals and opening customers' doors.

LESSON no. 2: Be ready to face cumbersome and stringent taxation regime. VAT payment and tax filing need to be done every month for the preceding month and no error must creep in tax computation and compliance. In case tax authorities file a complaint, 50% of the claim amount has to be paid before contesting it.

Post The Lessons

Having burnt our hands in the Transformer JV, we decided to set up the steel plant as a 100% owned subsidiary and no local partnership.

Initially, it seemed the right decision and served us well. But, soon, we realized that we had underestimated a few key risk areas. And they were the main drivers for my recommendation to exit the country.

The Board approved the Africa One steel project at the end of 2012, and Africa One Steel Manufacturing PLC (AOSM) was established in the year 2013 as a 100% foreign-owned private limited company for manufacturing Steel Billets and Rebars.

We acquired the required land in a prime industrial area and the corporate office was set up at the capital.

I approached the big banks in Africa One for term loans for part-financing the project. However, working with Banks in the country was proving difficult and inconvenient. Even after significant efforts over a long period we could not get the financing and we could not understand the reason for the delay in financial closure with our strong Group balance sheet.

Being an ex-Banker with a good initial career with ICICI and its subsidiaries in India, Corporate Banking has always been my forte. I simply could not understand and accept Africa One Banks dragging their feet and coming up with multiple queries on the project feasibility report. It was frustrating and displayed their limitations in structured project finance and knowledge the steel industry.

As we were large and reputed players in the middle east, I decided to arrange the required funds from Banks in the middle east, which were keen to expand their relationship with us. However, the Banks had a negative view on Africa One, and the financing had to be structured accordingly.

By the end of 2014, I had the Bank lines in place thru SMCL and achieved financial closure. The project was not delayed, as we were funding the initial expenditure thru internal accruals.

The project construction was progressing at a fast pace. We ordered the machinery and released the civil contracts. Based on Chairman's approval, I had transferred the entire equity contribution into the company's account with the Bank in Africa One.

First signs of trouble

October 2015. I land in capital of Africa One at 9.30 am on their national carrier for one of my routine visits. The only thing I liked about these visits was the African meals in Business Class. But I had a bad feeling about this visit. It was close to Diwali, and I wanted to be in India with my parents. My parents who live in India were old and I had to make frequent visits to their place (my father expired in 2018). My son, who has been my source of inspiration and the light of my life and lives in Canada with his mother also wanted me to visit Canada. They both are now Canadian nationals.

After reaching my base at the 5-star Hotel, I freshened up and rushed for my scheduled meeting with senior officials of the Central Bank of the country. I wore my best suit to get extra confidence even though my older suits too look fairly impressive in African environment. The agenda was to seek clarity on foreign currency allocation for import of machinery and subsequently for import of steel billets, the primary raw material needed for manufacturing rebars.

The country's political climate had rapidly deteriorated with an escalating tribal rivalry. Members of the fighting tribes were demanding equitable representation. This impacted business negatively. There was a sharp reduction in exports which led to an acute shortage of foreign currency, the precious US dollars.

Our GM of Africa One Steel accompanied me to the Bank but I asked him to be a silent participant as I wanted to be very focused in the meeting.

Something was waiting for me. The Central Bank threw the new rulebook at me. Then they slowly revealed their new directive for forex allocation. Priority was given to a set of import items & payments, on a first-come, first-served basis. The sectors were listed in order of priority and manufacturing was lower at 4th spot. Moreover, interest payments for foreign loans and for expat salaries, consultant fees are at the end of the priority list.

There was another rider. The Banks would allocate foreign currency to applicants under the above categories on a first-come, first served basis. They could take as much time as required to approve and if you did get the allocation, you were faced with a killer clause. The approved forex had to be utilized within 15 days. Several allocations were lapsing as companies and importers were unable to tie the import deals. The new guidelines meant that we would face trouble in getting forex for raw material import, expat salaries and in transferring dividends. Although we were banking with a leading Bank that met almost 70-75% of the nation's requirements, it did not matter.

I had dinner with our legal advisor who also filled me up with news on political crisis and the fact that emergency had been declared to counter the tribal violence. There were reports of some tribals getting into a manufacturing plant in one of the most troubled regions and killing some expat workers and staff. Our factory was in that zone. This was the first time I started getting worried about security environment in Africa One. Not for myself as I love flirting with danger and had been to ISIS infested Iraq in 2012 without any security. But I was worried about our steel plant workers especially the expats who would work there.

Our ED and I had also made a joint visit and with his tremendous expertise he too had made his independent assessment of the risks. CEO too had inputs from the GM in Africa One and had concerns on the risks.

We realised that immediate action was critical and advised the Chairman accordingly and it was decided to halt the project work. We were willing to wait and watch the political scenario and the economic conditions for a year. CEO, ED and I made regular quarterly visits to assess the situation on the ground.

Some two years back, it was clear that things were getting worse. However, the CEO was open to consider going ahead with the project as it would lead to company's growth. He and I probably had different view on Africa strategy like on few other issues.

In January 2017 Board meeting, I briefed the Board on the adverse business environment of the Africa One economy. I opined that maybe our steel venture in Africa one was an error. The Board was not convinced. They were still positive on the project. However, Chairman being an astute industrialist, had a better sense and advised me to revisit the area for a final re-assessment.

Four days in March.

This was possibly my 10th visit to the capital of Africa One. My final call was dependent upon this visit. I lined up meetings with senior officials from Government institutions, private sector industry leaders, bankers, lawyers and auditors.

These long and sometimes heated meetings allowed me to see the total picture.

The grim economic environment was getting further aggravated with famine. Foreign companies were exiting, given increasing country risks. An Indian company had abruptly decided to make a U-turn and exit their JV in which they had actually started acquiring 100% stake. Rumour doing the rounds said that a Gulf based company had also shelved their proposed steel project.

The forex problem was escalating and forex shortage was becoming worse. There was little hope of any improvement in the short or medium term. The drastic drop in USD inflows due to fall in exports, tourism and steep fall in inward remittances was driving it. During forced nationalization of the banks, the Africa One citizens settled abroad were forced to sell their holding at par value. It further choked limited remittances.

Yet, people including multi-country players like us were hoping for some improvement after the emergency period. We all expected Emergency to be lifted by end of the first quarter, but it got extended for a while.

Forex was being rationed. As our requirement of forex for Billet imports was relatively high and critical, the risk was too high.

Meeting with our Big4 and the Law firm

This was the last meeting I had. I requested the Managing Partner and owner of the law firm to hold it in his board room as I never liked the Big4 offices. The Lawyer's efficient secretary served excellent Macchiato, the Africa One coffee. I always thought I would ask the recipe from her but am disappointed that I never got around to it.

The partners of the law firm and the Audit firm were very well aware of our case. However, when I reiterated that we would need at least USD 4.0 million per month to meet our raw material import requirements, they were shocked at the size of our need. They knew that a few of their clients have been waiting for months for a few hundred thousand dollars. They shared cases where 1 million USD approvals had taken almost 1 year. There were Pharma companies (a priority sector) waiting for forex. And here we wanted 4.0 Million USD a month!

The Auditor pointed out that all manufacturing companies were keeping very high raw material inventory to tide over the delays and uncertainty in the availability of forex. And, if we tried doing so, it would severely impact our Operating costs.

As if that was not enough, he dropped the final straw. He told me that in the last 9 months, yes 9 months, the Banks had not approved or allotted any forex for imports of non-essential items to any private sector company.

There was no point in continuing with the meeting.

I had made up my mind and was completely convinced of my recommendation.

I closed my blue book with a bang. There was nothing more in the city for me to know. If I wanted to catch my flight, it was time for me to rush to the hotel and check out as fast as I could. But I knew that I will have to often come back to the capital of Africa One and find a potential buyer for the assets we had stopped working with.

....

"Sir, would you like to have an African meal?" The pretty crew member of Africa One business class broke my chain of thought.

I had just finished writing my note to the Board and forwarded it to my secretary with a request to type and keep it on my desk first thing in the morning.

"Yes," I said, "That would be very nice"

I knew I would be able to convince the Chairman and the Board to take a significant loss to shield from future losses.

· ·

I made a mental note of things to look at in any foreign investment. I realize the importance of a detailed understanding. It is better to take time than to jump into action, as you need to manage a spectrum of risks including:

Political/Sovereign risk: Political instability, effects of Emergency, etc.; and how these will affect the general investment climate and resultant economic growth.

Currency Risk: Likely depreciation of local currency will erode profits in USD terms. So budget the returns in USD terms after factoring in adequate depreciation.

Forex Availability Risk: This is the largest risk factor especially if raw material has to be imported.

Funds Transfer Risk: One may encounter restrictions on the transfer of money even for serving foreign loans, dividends, expat salaries, consultant/professional fees.

The Banyan Tree Agency

Sanjeev Kotnala

It is the early 1990s, mobile and pagers are still a few years away. Fax and telex are your communication lifelines. There is some loose talk about things like pagers and mobiles, but they are yet to hit the scene. The artwork in Studios is made manually by a skilled set of artists. Photography shoots are detailed with not much margin for error. It is costly to make corrections on a system that has just made its entry. The seniors have started getting a personal computer, and the electric typewriters are slowly on the way out.

It is an early part of my professional life, and I work in one of India's largest Advertising agencies. I recently moved from Mudra, Ahmedabad to HTA; Hindustan Thompson Associates. The Delhi branch address was interesting. HTA, above ball bearing market, 36 Rani Jhansi road, Jhandewalon. The New generation knows HTA as JWT.

Agency business had four strong pillars in those days. Client Servicing which was the king at that time and dictated terms; Creative which was the central part; Account Planning which believed it was the architect of brand success with inputs on consumer insights; and then there was Media, where agency earned commissions. In between were administration and finance and Studio. Before I wrap this up, let me share something important. The Studio was one of the most critical departments. It controlled the pace of the agency as it defined the number of artworks that got finished in a day.

It was still the era of legitimate, decent 15% commission. In spite of that, the best of the agencies ran tight ships with substantial control over expenses. The size of the agency was still the function of its media billing. The fight was always about, which is the largest agency.

HTA was great when it came to financial controls. There were systems in place to help ease out things. There were Monday Morning Meetings (MMM), which helped to prioritise jobs at the Studio or with the creative teams. It was where inter-department and Intra-department commitments were enforced. In the absence of WhatsApp and group- emails, this was what kept the teams on the same page. It was also the first stage check on financials.

Here one of the critical discussion used to be the financial health of the agency. Things of vital importance were a list of estimates pending for approval with the Client. These were minutely segregated by age, department and value and then discussed threadbare. Another thing that was seriously considered was revenue (bill raised) and collection (Bill Paid).

In fact, HTA in the period of financial crunch would follow the policy called, 'Cheque in or check out'. In case you failed to collect the payment from the Client, you can check out of the office (in fact don't come in) and check-in at the client office with no job but the sole idea of embarrassing him to make the payment. No jokes, I have seen it in operation.

This story focusses on the revenue estimation- the estimate approval part of the business. In the agency business, when jobs were initiated, parallelly estimates were generated. As a principle, the estimate was supposed to be approved much before the work began. However, most of the time, clients approved them mid-way or even after the job was finished.

I was in the client servicing department. One of the accounts I was servicing was ITC Welcomgroup, the hotel chain. In ITC Welcomgroup, the list of unapproved estimates was growing steadily. And many of them were too old. In every Monday morning meeting, I used to walk through a minefield of questions. New excuses were being invented with regularity. I was somehow managing to camouflage my team and my inability to bring down the number of unapproved estimates.

My Group leader was Jagdip Bakshi (JB). In the Monday morning meetings, he saw my hesitation and discomfort. He knew that the unapproved estimate situation in ITC Welcomgroup situation was way beyond acceptable. However, in the meeting, he used to avoid pointing it out, but question me separately on the subject. The twitch of the raised eyebrow was enough to signal his displeasure. One made the regular promise of cleaning the ness by the next Sunday, fully aware that there was no way anything was going to happen.

After a few Mondays, when one was having no excuse, one started missing the ritualistic Monday Morning Meeting. That was not the solution, as JB would then ask you for detail later in the day.

It was this period when JB decided to take the problem head-on.

He asked me to get all the estimates ready in triplicate. That's how the estimate sets were made. The concept of self carbon paper was restricted to very important documents. Simply said, the Client has to sign every copy of the estimate, or we used to physically insert the carbon paper form estimate set to another. The Client retained the first copy. Two copies came back to the agency. One went to records and second to the studio/finance for future processing.

So, that day, he asked me to set up a meeting with the Client the next day. He said, just say JB wants a courtesy meeting. No Agenda. I don't remember who was at the client end.

Setting up meetings at ITC Welcome group was straightforward. Next day was Tuesday when anyway we were supposed to have the weekly meeting. The meeting venue was the annexe behind the main Maurya Sheraton building in the diplomatic estate.

At the appointed hour, Jagdip Bakshi and I walked into the client office. I was carrying all the estimate. In the night, I had gone through each of the estimates and was ready to answer any question. I knew exactly the reason for which they remained unapproved.

For a large part of the scheduled 30 minutes, Jagdip did not even bring the question of estimates approvals. It was okay with me, as I was definitely not interested in the discussion. However, I knew this was the best opportunity that I should not miss out. Hence, I was using every non-verbal communication trick to ask Jagdip what was happening. I was sure Jagdip had some trick up his sleeve. He had previously also surprised me in similar situations, I will share some other time.

So, when there were some 5-10 minutes left for the meeting to get over, Jagdip signalled me to get the estimates out. In a flash, I dropped some 60 plus estimates on the table.

Jagdip's tone changed. It lost its socialising edge.

So JB addresses the Client and in a matter of fact says, 'Hey, by the way, there are these estimates which have been pending- I thought I would get them approved.'

ITC Guy smiled and said 'But JB these are too high.'

JB smiled and said nothing. As if he understands.

In his characteristic way, he started on a tangent. I did not initially make out what he was driving at.

'Hey, know I was here last night at your coffee shop, at around 10 in the night. I had a beer, and it cost some Rupees 230. Worse you guys did not even think of taking off the price tag on the bottle that told me that it was only Rs 20 outside. What a rip off.'

ITC Guy took the bait. 'What did you expect JB. You were in the finest 5 stars, we give you a beer at the temperature it should be. You pay for the ambience, structure, waiter serving you, AC; all of them are an investment and you in your Rs 230 are paying for all of it.'

JB Smiled and went for the kill 'yeah yeah, maybe we are not the best agency. Maybe we don't need to give our employees such comfort. Maybe you think they sit under the banyan tree out in the open and they don't get AC and... you know when you get the best to work for you... you also end up paying for that service and talent."

ITC guy slowly pulled the pile of estimates and signing each and every copy without any questions.

The agency under Banyan Tree won the day.

Tsunami Discovery

Girish Patarphod

The year 2004. I remember it was a few interesting things. Britney, the pop star, was married twice. Once to Kevin Federline, with whom she had two sons, and once to Jason Alexander, which was annulled days later. Janet Jackson's breast became exposed during the Super Bowl halftime show featuring Jackson and Justin Timberlake, prompting debate about the moral standards of American broadcast networks. Facebook was launched, and the serial 'Friends' last episode was aired. And towards the end of the year, on Dec. 26, The tsunami's struck after a massive earthquake hit a fault line running under the sea, killing more than 230,000 people.

What you don't know is what I discovered that year as part of an assignment. There was this consultancy assignment we signed with a large conglomerate (LC) having over USD 20 billion in assets. They had established a wholly-owned subsidiary as a start-up to provide web-based services in Mumbai. They had already infused close to 60 million USD in the start-up. The start-up was bleeding profusely. The LC, in not so unexpected move, had summarily sacked everyone who was a Vice-president and above and sent a new MD from head office to take charge. I was a part of the new team.

I spent the initial three months trying to get the grip of the situation. One of the focus areas was how the business was conducted? And second, working closely with the crack audit team sent by Head Office. We were looking closely into all transactions. We wanted to plug all leakages and make a difference.

During our audit, I discovered something strange. The start-up had placed orders for massive computers and associated software with a select few international giants. The consignment was already delivered, and now all of these computers and hardware were lying unused. On top of that, all the specialised and customised software was not put to some real productive applications. The matter was not only surprising but beat every possible logic. Several millions of dollars were figuratively burnt.

I naturally raised the issue with my counterpart with the LC. I then took the matter up to the Managing Director of the LC. And, I was politely told to back off, and concentrate on other issues.

I backed off. A part of me presumed that it was a part of corporate financial malfeasance that one hears about so often these days. My assignment finished in a few years.

And then came 2011. Now, this was the year you remember for one-of-the strongest earthquakes, of magnitude 8.9, triggering a 10 metre-high tsunami, that sweeps away homes, vehicles and crops in Japan. The hunt for US enemy number one- Osama bin Laden ends with his encounter at Abbottabad, Pakistan. Muammar Gaddafi, the 'king of kings,' dies in his hometown. Steve **Jobs**, the founder and former CEO of Apple, loses his battle to Pancreatic Cancer. What you don't know is what I discovered in 2011.

After that discovered misuse of assets and my finishing the assignment, I began a consulting relationship with the same LC. This lasted for several years.

Then I remember this party. It is etched on my mind. It was like one of those of corporate parties where tongues tend to get loose as the night progresses. And discretion is thrown to the winds in some game of one-up-man-ship where people start boasting and sharing what they should best keep to themselves.

It was a party in one of the top floors of a decent swank boutique hotel. There was a celebration for some milestone achieved. People were dressed in their best, and the show had some artist from Bollywood also performing.

I was at the large enough terrace enjoying the view and engaging one of the LC executives in conversation. He was a bit tipsy but holding on to his drink. I don't know how our conversation meandering through the various uninteresting topics landed to the LC subsidiary which was supposed to provide web service in Mumbai. Here, is when I got to know the real inside story behind the unused computer and the specialised custom software.

Now, this the way things panned out.

The LC had purchased a large tract of land. A few hundred acres of it, all at a throwaway price. This land had a connectivity problem and was considered to be in the middle of no-where. There they built a few towers. Then the LC targeted few international companies and placed lucrative orders with them. There was an unwritten understanding that these global companies would have offices in these towers. Once several large players occupied the offices, everyone wanted to be at this new happening address. The LC then convinced the government to build connectivity with this land which was in the middle of no-where. In a decade or so, this became a mega business hub and had most of the known big companies with offices in those towers. Then, as planned, the LC sold off the adjoining land in bits and pieces at an ever spiralling rate.

The whole story stunned me. Poor me, I simply could not see the moves. I could not understand the game.

It was now clear, why I was discouraged from probing what I thought was a brilliant discovery of wastage and misappropiration. Something, inside me never wanted to believe the story. So, I went back and did my own bit of investigation- I was disappointed to find enough evidence that said, the story was absolutely right. And my guess, the LC ended up making close to 700 million USDs on the initial USD 690 million infusions.

And now I know, why all the VP plus level were summarily sacked. How the charade was brilliantly played out to further pull the wool over the happenings. Between the two Tsunami years, I learnt two things. One, unexpected discoveries could be pre-planned, and two, things that don't glitter could still be gold.

SECTION-B
People

Life Is Not About Giving Up

S M Sundaram

Some lessons in life are so imprinted in your mind that you can relive them again and again. I was about 12 years old, visiting my grandparents in Chennai during the summer holidays. I had lived in Ashok Nagar with them till 5th standard and had many friends in the local colony. It was also where my cricket and badminton skills were born and honed. With friends ranging from college-going boys to elementary school kids, it was truly a melting pot of ages and cultures, and a hub of camaraderie.

Cricket, as you can well imagine, was as much de rigueur in the 1970s as it is today. Having a set of sticks for wickets at one end was luxury enough. At the other end was invariably a brick which acted as a 'wicket' to effect run-outs or a marker to tell the bowler the line he couldn't cross. There was also just one bat, which meant the 'runner' or non-striker was not burdened with any paraphernalia.

Forget about a cricket ball. Even a tennis ball was a luxury. A multi-coloured rubber ball bought for 25 paise. That too contributed by all those who could throw 5 paise each into the common pool. It probably lasted about a week before it got impaled on one of the barbed wire fences surrounding the playground, requiring the next round of pooling of money.

This was the background for one of those crucial matches with the team that lived in the neighbouring locality. For a 12-year, every game was important. The enthusiasm and the desire to be always on the winning side was high. It could very well have been an India-Pakistan match.

The game went pretty much like any other game. The 'visiting' side won the toss and - Surprise! Surprise! - batted first!! They piled on about 60+ runs before losing all their wickets.

Our side began chase with gusto. 20…30…40… almost all out, except for the last pair at the wicket. 20+ more runs to get. Might as well have been 100+ in today's context with no. 6 and no.11 at the crease. I was that no. 11 – at the non-striker's end. My friend Satish, much older than me and our team's star batsman was on strike – and so long as he was around, hope still lingered. Like any other 'tween, the only thing that interested me was my batting. I was always interested in batting. You waited and wanted to be at the other end where the action was. Irrespective of what my batting prowess or the opposition's strength was.

Satish hit one of those loose deliveries hard. It was a brilliant straight drive. High elbow; front foot pointing in the direction of the shot; all along the ground. I saw the ball going past the bowler now on his follow-through. I knew there was a run in it and a chance for me to bat rest of the over. Without even looking at where the ball went, I ran full tilt - only to find myself moments later nose-to-nose with Satish at the striker's end! Eskimos may greet each other by rubbing noses, but what I got from Satish was more of a horrified stare.

What the hell! Satish hadn't budged!! As I looked back, I realized there was a good reason for him to stay rooted to his crease. The ball had not gone far. There was a fielder stationed 3 feet behind the bowling crease, and he was holding the ball now. How could I have missed seeing him?

He could have run me out any one of 3 ways. Walked over to the single brick at the bowler's end and just stepped on it or touched it with the ball. Tossed the ball to the bowler, to do the honours, or hand over the ball to the bowler to … you get the picture.

Not sure what got into my head, but I just turned around and ran back towards the non-striker's end, where I had come from and from where I had no business moving in the first place. It was a do or die situation. You don't get to bat if you are out. I run marathons, but I don't think I ever ran that earnestly or ever that fast in my life. All this while being blissfully unaware of a totally different game going on between the bowler and fielder. They were clearly in two minds.

Seeing how close the fielder was to the bowler, he stretched out his hand to pass on the ball. The bowler had a different expectation or understanding of what should be done; he expected the fielder to throw the ball. Hence he pouched his hands in a 'ready to catch' mode.

Realizing the bowler had something different in mind, the fielder now prepared to toss the ball to the bowler, who had meanwhile reached out with his hand to take the ball from the fielder's hand.

Like some bizarre tribal ritual or cosmic dance, the bowler and fielder continued to play this tango a few times. They had no idea that I was hurtling like a runaway missile in their direction. Maybe they thought they had all the time in the world to run me out. I, of course, knew nothing of any of this goings-on. I was only interested in reaching the safety of the crease at the non-striker's end.

Though it felt like eons, all this played out over just a few moments. Those few seconds was all it took for my passionate, headlong, unthinking, mad dash to deposit me back to the safety of the crease at the bowler's end.

No one could believe what had just happened. It was too weird and too quick for anyone's brain to comprehend.

How could I NOT be out?! While the fielding side howled in exasperated frustration, the bowler and fielder looked disbelievingly bewildered. All types of curses and swear words flew around. Meanwhile, my team members were laughing their heads off, with me on the ground doing what would today be called ROFLMAO!

What followed was almost sedate in comparison to this incident. I picked myself up from the dusty ground. Took me a few more minutes to stop laughing. But we could see that suddenly, the back and the spirit of the fielding side had been broken. The spring in their stride had vanished. Satish and I knocked off the 20+ runs that we needed to win. It was almost that we were pre-ordained to win that day! And a 12-year old become a hero in the midst of a bunch of college and high-school going kids.

Much later, as I ruminated on what had transpired, I realized more than the few extra overs I got to bat or the runs I scored, the biggest gain from the day was a lesson for life. DON'T GIVE UP. You are only responsible for the efforts you make; results may or may not be on your side.

With non-existent odds, I had pulled off a heist.

That day, I learned never to throw in the towel, however hopeless or bleak the situation may be. Many a time in both my professional career and personal life, this lesson became one of the most applied learnings. Be it during my academic career or when I was in a start-up amidst one of the worst recessions, we were hanging in not by our fingertips, but by the tips of our fingernails. Survive we did. Just as I had on that fateful day as a 12-year-old. Some lessons are learnt and forgotten. Others are seared and branded into one's memory so much that they become a part of what we are and defines who we are and who we become.

A New City,
A New Language

S Subramanian

Until 1982, when I completed my bachelor's degree in engineering from the College of Engineering, Madras, I had only travelled between the two states Kerala and Tamil Nadu. And a few detours into Nellore district in Andhra Pradesh, adjacent to Chennai. I was fluent in Malayalam, Tamil and English. I could read Hindi haltingly but did not understand the language at all.

I secured an opening as Service Engineer in Madras in a reputed Bombay headquartered company. As a new recruit, I was sent to Mumbai for a three-month training stint after a couple of months of fieldwork at Chennai. The onus of finding suitable boarding and lodging in Bombay was on me for which an extra monthly allowance was provided by my employer. I had no problem on this score as I knew some people in Bombay.

My trials and tribulations with a new language, Hindi, started on my way to Bombay on Dadar Express. A vendor was selling long tender pale green vegetable "*kakdi*" in the train. I was coming across this vegetable for the first time. By the time I found out from another traveller that "*kakdi*" was a variety of cucumber, the vendor had moved two coaches ahead. I caught up with the vendor, but I was left tongue-tied as he was conversing in Hindi. I followed till a passenger negotiated with the vendor, paid and bought some pieces. I handed over the amount of money to the vendor and bought "*kakdi*" without uttering a word! For a man of many words and long sentences in the languages I am good at, faced with a new language, it was a swing to the other extreme of the pendulum for me.

I initially stayed in Santa Cruz with a family friend. I had travelled long distance on local trains in Madras almost daily for twelve years in Chennai but soon realised that experience was of no consequence in local train travel in Bombay. The trains were so crowded, the passengers were packed like sardines. Even if I wanted to put my hand in my pocket, I would have ended up picking somebody else's pocket. Most of the time, I was standing on someone else's toes, or my toes were bearing the load of someone else. Unfamiliarity with the local train system once made me inadvertently travel by ladies compartment and suffer detention at Railway Police station at Dadar. I presented myself at railway magistrate's court at Bombay VT station and was fined twenty-five rupees for the infraction. In a lighter vein, I told the Dadar railway police sub-inspector my punishment was unfair as there were no ladies in the compartment I boarded. The sub-inspector reciprocated in an equally jovial manner. He said, in future, he would ensure there were ladies around when he apprehended me.

Local train travel experience in Bombay will not be complete without a brief statement on Dadar station where Central and Western Railways converge before branching out. The overhead gangways in this station were as broad as national highways and were very crowded. Once on the gangway, any first-timer to Dadar station would have to be a genius to locate the right platform for his local train.

I reached our office well in time on the first day.

I had memorised Hindi numbers up to twenty and after that in multiples of five before I embarked on the first journey to Mumbai. This was not much help in the office, and factory premises as those serving subsidised vadaa pav, bread omelette and tea spoke only Marathi. My first attempt to buy breakfast left me foxed. I was asked to pay *pannaas* paise. I gave him a rupee and he returned the change. This transaction practically taught me *pannaas* meant fifty.

I was left to my own devices with a schedule of training at various plants in the company premises situated in a suburb of Bombay. A week into the training, I realised the futility of standing around and staring at machines the whole day. With nobody to mentor me, my sole aim during training turned to fill my stomach. I would report in the morning on time and feast on the vada paav / bread omelette breakfast. Time slowly crept towards lunch break. After lunch, I used to leave the factory premises and roam around places which caught my fancy. I spent a week each in the factories of each product group.

I boarded buses going into the city and used to buy a ticket to the destination mentioned on the display board. Not sure where I would get down, this was the safest thing to do to be on the right side of the law in case of a surprise ticket check.

The first such roaming trip was on a double-deck bus to Backbay Depot. I secured a seat on the first row on the upper deck. After travelling for more than an hour, I suddenly saw tall buildings to my right at a reasonable distance. I knew the clutch of buildings was at Nariman Point from the photos on Bombay in newspapers and magazines. I immediately rushed down and wanted to alight, but the bus was passing through a long straight road with no stops in the vicinity. I jumped out of the bus when it slowed at a turning and proceeded on foot to Nariman Point.

On another occasion, I alighted at a locality which had a lot of shops and some modern buildings. It was near Worli, and after roaming around the place, I decided to go home only to realise that I had alighted from the bus on a one-way road. I had a tough time locating the bus stop in the opposite direction. I tried to figure out who in public would respond to my query in English but drew a blank when I popped my question. After this experience, whenever I got down mid-way on my "roaming" trips, I alighted only after making sure that buses were plying on the other side of the road too!

While waiting at bus stops and railway stations, some people used to ask me for the time of the day. I used to be in short-sleeved shirts and was a sitting duck for such queries. I could count spontaneously in Hindi up to five but for any number beyond I had to start counting in Hindi mentally from one. Then the choice of "sava", "sade" and "pouney" had to be grappled with. So once I zeroed in on a response, I used to stick to the time I blurted out first. So in the whole journey for anybody asking me the time would get the stock response!

A month into my training, somebody noticed that I was wearing my watch only after reaching the office and was pocketing it before leaving the office. He was curious to know the reason.

Once in the local bus, I was seated next to someone in a typical rural outfit including the headgear. He asked me the time of the day. Wanting to give my Hindi "search" engine a much-needed rest, I showed him my watch dial so that he could read the time for himself. But he did not know to read my watch and wanted me to tell him the time. For the rest of my training stint, I did not wear my watch in public!

I had to go "out of the way" to learn an important verb in Hindi. I was travelling in an auto-rickshaw in Thane. The driver pulled over at a secluded spot and asked me something which sounded like a request for permission. I nodded wondering what he was up to. He got down, pulled out his sacred thread from beneath his shirt and wrapped a part of it around his ear in the process splashing the verb "peshaab" into my memory.

Some of my college mates had taken up jobs in Mumbai in some reputed companies, and they too were poor in Hindi. We used to get together and roam around the city on holidays. We bought some goods from pavement vendors but found the process of negotiation tough. If the vendor dropped the price from forty rupees to say, thirty-two or twenty-seven rupees, we would walk away. Chances of striking a deal were better for the vendor if he had told thirty-five or thirty. All of us knew numbers in Hindi beyond twenty in only multiples of five!

Our favourite haunt was Colaba- Nariman Point- Backbay- Ballard Pier area and we covered this stretch on foot. When tired, we used to take rest in the lobby of Oberoi and Taj Mahal Hotels!

One could order a pot of tea for ten rupees at the Coffee Shop in Taj Mahal hotel those days. We used to nurse a couple of pot of tea and hang around the coffee shop as long as outermost limits of decency were about to be breached.

Our group was from conservative backgrounds and boys-only schools. We keenly observed several young women in skirts in the downtown area. Most of them used buses and shared taxis into and out of Churchgate and Mumbai VT stations. We chose to sit one per row in buses from terminus on our roaming trips with the fond hope some "young persons" would find us good company. We had no such luck despite repeated attempts on different bus routes leading to the local train terminal stations.

Another favourite pastime was gawking at young couples holding hands, legs, cheeks and more in the benches at Paanch gardens Dadar and Bandra sea face. We were pictures of concentration on such occasions. One of those days at Paanch gardens, we found one in our group suddenly missing. We looked around and saw him standing at some distance. We wondered what made him feel shy suddenly and move away. He had seen his boss and spouse on one of the park benches directly in front of us and had just disappeared. Since our bosses were not around, we let him sulk and went back to gawking.

On completion of training, I returned to Chennai with far more positive experiences than negative ones with the new language and the new city. I was the first among my close friends to spend time in Bombay. For several days, my recollections of Bombay days kept them entertained.

I have stayed and worked in several cities all over India. My skill in conversational Hindi is now more than enough to get work done and strike social conversations. As the years flew by, new places and new people did not daunt me. I enjoy being in new places among new people. It all started with the Mumbai experience.

Driving A Positive Mindset

Kumar Ekambaram

It was in the year 1980. I joined NDDB as a trainee engineer and after about three years, in 1983-84 had the opportunity of working on a prestigious project of erecting and commissioning the first Aseptic Packaging Plant for treated milk in India, at Surat Dairy. This packed milk would have a shelf life of 60 days without refrigeration. This plant was imported and erected under the supervision of the manufacturers of the machine who were the pioneers in Aseptic Packaging plants and the largest player globally. Aseptically packaged milk was to be test-launched in India for the first time after which the plan was to launch it nationally.

I was working along with the Packaging Machine engineers from Europe, and we were taking test trials. One evening just two days before the test launch, there was some issue. The Engineers from Europe left the packaging station site without any information and flew out of the country. Being very junior in the organisation and relatively new in the corporate set up, I had no idea what should be my course of action. Just three hours after the European engineers had left, I received a call on the landline (no mobile those days). It was from the corporate office, and the M.D. of the company wanted to talk to the Engineer in charge of the Packaging Machines. As I was the senior-most, I had to attend the call much against my wishes.

With my mind racing with all possible answers without knowing the question, I picked up the phone. I was greeted with silence from the other end. And then suddenly there was firm but polite voice enquiring, "are you the person in charge of the packaging machine from our side", and to this, I answered affirmatively. He asked me whether I knew that the European engineers had left. I said, "yes this afternoon" thinking this was easy as I had the answer little realising that this was only a leading question.

Then the question came "can you run the machine for packing the milk for test launch". Out of the blue, here was a situation I was not prepared for. Neither the question, nor for taking the responsibility of running the packaging machine. So I tried to navigate my way with some vague answers. I was definitely not saying" yes" as I had no confidence. And I was afraid to say "no" as I might get sacked. After listening to my replies, The MD said, "Young man I just want a simple answer "Yes" or "No" from you". I thought for a quick moment and said" Yes" as it gave me some time. He said "thank you and all the best for the test launch" and cut the phone.

I had 48 hours before the first batch of Aseptically Packaged Milk would be ready for a test launch, a landmark event in the annals of the Indian Dairy Industry. In those 48 hours, I had to find a way to salvage the situation.

I was working in Gujarat. Those days there was only a weekly direct train to my home town. Yes, one of the options I was looking was to abandon the site but decided against it as my original documents were with the company. Before I knew the "D day" had come and the production was scheduled for 7.30 AM. The plan was to keep the milk packet samples after the production for testing in lab before they were cleared for launch in the market.

We started the production as scheduled. I was running the machine with butterflies in my stomach. As time went by the production pressure made me forget all the fears, and I was fully involved in the production. After 3 hours of production run, we took out the samples needed for testing. We sent it to the lab for the physical check. After getting the green signal, we dispatched the first truck containing the first batch of Aseptically Packed Milk to the market, which was about 3 hours from the factory. The results of the bacterial quality check would take 2 to 3 days, so though I was happy after the despatch, I was still tense. The milk was to be stored in the outlets we had chosen to distribute the milk and then given to the selected customers whom we had identified for the test launch exercise. After we got the news that the truck had reached the destination, we felt a bit relaxed little realising that our nightmare was about to begin.

Next morning went to the packaging station eagerly to find out the results from the quality department and the news was not very encouraging as a few packets of milk curdled. The entire day we waited for some news from the market. We received no communication from the distributors, which we took it for good news but the truth as we learnt later was the distributors did not know what to look for in the faulty packs hence they had not reverted. It was the following day the tsunami struck – quite a few of the milk packets with the distributors had curdled.

We were wondering what to do. The quality person put it jokingly "it's a new process of getting curd to market" however I was in no mood for such jokes. Sometime late that evening the landline rang. I felt it was my death bell ringing. As expected, the call was from the headquarters asking for the head of quality, Milk production, packaging and marketing to come down to head office the next day. It was a day I would never forget as the next day was the day of the week when there was a direct train to my home town. I called my roommate and told him of the debacle and said that I had been summoned to the head office and was sure that I would get the pink slip. I also told him to pack my belongings and bring it to the station as the train to my home town was to depart at 19.00 Hrs and I would not have time to come home to pack and leave.

This was my frame of mind when we went to the head office. All of us were in the same mindset; only the degree differed depending on one's experience. I was the junior-most.

The corporate office was about 3 hours journey by train from the packaging station. As we boarded the train for once I was praying that the train would be late, but as luck would have it the train arrived on time and we entered the corporate office at 10.30 Hrs. On our arrival, the receptionist told us to wait in the waiting room with the M.D., and we waited there. The feeling was somewhat like lambs waiting at the slaughterhouse. After about 15 minutes, we were taken to his office. Our M.D., a man in his late 50's, welcomed us and asked us to take our seat. After exchanging pleasantries, he asked us individually to detail our experience of the test launch exercise. All of us stumbled through our experiences. Every one of us cleverly, keeping away from what went wrong. In the course of our discussion, he asked us a few pointed questions like

- Was the production run as per the parameters specified by the company?
- Did you have any break in the production run?
- Were the milk crates loaded and stacked firmly in the truck?
- What was the road condition of the route taken?
- Did any of you travel with the truck?
- Did the truck stop in between in the route?

- Were the milk crates unloaded safely from the truck?
- What were the conditions in which the milk crates were stored at the distributers end?
- Did all the distributors complain about curdled milk?
- What was the physical state of the milk packets?

We had some answers but realised that they lacked the content needed to find a solution to the problem at hand.

I'm sure he must have sensed our feelings from our expressions and answers. He said, "*I understand you guys are feeling sorry that the test launch did not go well. But tell me wasn't the test launch suppose to throw up all the weak links, isn't that the purpose of doing a test launch exercise*". He continued, "*there is no reason to feel sorry. However, what makes me feel bad is that none of you even hinted at the solutions. I presume it is because you did not know the problems that were the cause for the milk getting curdled inside the packs*. Finally, he concluded in a firm voice. "*I suggest you go back and try to identify all the problems and then work on the solution and I'm sure we will be ready with our product for the final launch*". With this the meeting came to an end and we trooped out of his office with feelings which were a mixture of relief, disbelief, happiness, disappointment, motivation, etc.

We had come to the meeting expecting to be reprimanded, fired etc. and there was not a single mention made of it. On the contrary we were encouraged to fix the problem and get ready for the final launch.

After leaving the office, we sat down at the Chai shop outside the office, each one waiting for the other person to break the silence. Finally, I cut the silence with my question "when is our train to the milk packaging centre". All our minds were so preoccupied with our meeting we decided to go to railway station and wait. Finally we boarded the train at 15.30 Hrs and

I quickly chose a single seat by the window, as I was in no mood for conversation. As the train chugged out of the station, my mind was flooded with the day's happenings. I started to go through the scenes frame by frame, slowly reflecting on each interaction that happened in the office. I was reasonably sure that others were also in the same reflective mood.

We met the next day and drew up our action plan. The energy in the meeting room was high, with each one going into great detail to identify the problem, and discussing the solution. An action plan was drawn, implemented, and in a month, the product was launched and was accepted well by the market.

After the launch, I sat back, wanting to identify what it was that drove us to this success. Of course, it was the team's hard work but underneath all this was the positive mindset driven into each of us by the short and focused meeting with the M.D. where he demonstrated the following traits

1. Focused on the issue
2. Did not humiliate anyone in front of others
3. Never once put into us the fear of failure
4. Showed us the direction to success
5. Gave us the confidence that he was backing us in this project.

In my more than three decades of professional career, the above five golden rules have always come to my rescue. When I had to motivate and energise the team or when their spirits were down. This meeting with the M.D. and the learning's were a game-changer in my life. Thank You, Sir.

The Parable of the UniMuni

S. Ram Kumar

A few years ago, more than a mid-life crisis, I was assailed by pathological doubt. I saw where my neighbours, friends, relatives and CLASSMATES were. And their kids, cars, houses, vacations, dogs and all else. "Where am I?" was nagging me intensely. And it is not just keeping up with the Joneses. Magnificently more amplified. My IIMA PGP '87 cohort, as you will read elsewhere in the book is full of spectacular over-performers. My school classmate's daughter, PV Sindhu, is a world-class gold winner in Badminton. Hell, my students have made millions in selling startups. And where was I?

And then the demons of rationalisation torment and assuage. 'Their' success is due to luck, a well-connected family, underhand tactics, genetics...anything that I cannot be held responsible for. Sickening.

And so I searched. For something that I alone would be responsible for. A social experiment like, you know, from school chemistry – something is proportional to another provided all else is constant? Is there one? Is such an experiment accessible? What? How? What on earth could it be where I and I alone would be responsible for success or failure. No strings attached. What kind of miracle would such a thing be?

And then the miracle happened. I found unicycles. A single wheel, a pair of pedals and a seat. It turned into an insatiable obsession. And this is the sledgehammer style learning that Unicycling delivered to me.

. . . .

I got a Taiwan made, 'cheapo' rig from Singapore and then life or learning has never been the same.

I have spent decades with wheels and tracks. Been there done that. My list includes simple bicycles, car, motorcycles, truck, 4X4, 6X6, road roller, grader, backhoe, bulldozer and even stuff like roller skates, in-line skates and stilts. You can't fault me in thinking it was going to be a breeze - sledgehammer surprise. The work of the Devil – the Unicycle is insanely difficult.

Unicycling is very simple. There are only two possibilities.

You stay on top of the damn thing OR not to let the bugger get away from under you. No one can help you. Not your parents, astrologers, tantriks, soothsayers, gurujis, that uncle who is in a top government post, father-in-law, banker, accountant, oracles or the Ouija board. No one can advise you. It makes NO difference. Stay on top or prevent the Unicycle sliding out.

It looked impossible when I first saw the Unicycle. Even after seeing someone else ride it, it seemed impossible, counterintuitive and magical

After spending some time trying to ride the damn thing. I started questioning why the hell I was doing so.

Unicycling has no practical application. It is not a 'recognised' sport. Even scientific studies suggest that it is the most inefficient form of transport. There is virtually nothing to adjust, to get a sense of control – just pedals, a seat and a wheel...

Some learn in hours - some learn it in months - some never manage to get the ride going. I took three long months.

It was clear to me; It is ONLY between you and your Unicycle – always. It does not matter if you are rich or poor, educated

or uneducated. Or literate or illiterate (yes one can be literate but uneducated). You can come from generations of statesmen or have a lineage of crushing ordinariness. Landed or labour class. Knighted or wretched. King, knight, slave, samurai, thief or saint. Your caste, creed, colour, language or origin, nothing matters. Your history doesn't matter. Who you are doesn't matter. What matters is what you want and your willingness to give it a go.

The surprising thing about Unicycles is that they give no feedback. With every other thing I have learnt from masonry to cooking, you do get a sense of when you are getting warmer. This thing is wicked. You can try 890 times to get on, and you feel you are just as bad as at try# 1. Then bam !!!! You are on !!! It takes an enormous amount of faith to persevere.

Everything is counterintuitive. Whatever you knew is useless. The wheels are direct drive. There is NO freewheel. There are no brakes, and there are no handles. And what you are trying to achieve is not to stay on top. What you are trying is incredibly counter to every instinct. You are trying to fall forward and control it. Essentially it is a continuous series of controlled falls that you are trying to recover from – continuously. That's front and back. And both sides too.

You can be strong or weak. Male or female or in between. Tall or short. Big or small. Beautiful or plug-ugly. Your physique or your looks don't matter. You may be bright and sharp. Or you can buy your way to education. Perhaps your 'history' or surname exceptionally entitles you. Your family name; Gates, Buffett, Rothschild, Guggenheim, Gandhi or Hitler doesn't matter. **It is ONLY between you and your Unicycle – always. And how resilient you are.**

The repeated attempts to learn to ride the Unicycle saps the body and soul and keeps them totally occupied. It takes just a nanosecond for things to happen. You let your thoughts wander for a microsecond, and you have a UPD – Unicycling euphemism for UnPlanned Dismount — a fall. And by the way, even the fall is inglorious, for your feet are only a few inches from the ground, and your speed is virtually nothing !!!!

To succeed, you have to be constant into the process and nowhere else. To me, it is a form of ultra-disciplined meditation. There is no instruction manual, and no one can teach you. All the work is in achieving muscle memory, heightening proprioception and focus. The headaches, and so does the body. Thighs, calves, ankles, hips and shoulders weep for deliverance and feel like jelly for hours.

Your Unicycle couldn't care less. Your caste and country: Boston or otherwise Brahmin, all parts of Manu's classification, Blue, green, Black, Yellow Pink - blood or skin. Your dynasty cannot help. In sports or even films, army or politics, business or terrorism, god, man or evil tyrant....dynasty rules, maybe. But never around unicycles. It is ONLY between you and your Unicycle – always. And what can help is your will, pushing you not to leave it half done. You will not accept defeat before the race is over.

The best, the best well-wishers or even experts told me is some feeble stuff like, Sit on the seat. Insane as it sounds, this is extremely difficult to do. Sit straight and look ahead !!!! That's it. That's all there is to it.

The obsession with learning is narcotic in its intensity. I often dreamt about it. I woke up and could not wait to get to my next session. I realised, if I miss a few sessions, it is likely I will have to start all over again.

Unlike in many other things I learnt, in case of Unicycling, I learnt to hate the youtube videos. Watching the pros is to die every frame. They are truly outstanding.

And then one day, ONE DAY it happened. I get on top and achieve two whole revolutions. The high is hard to describe.

And then people ask me whether you plan to be in the circus? Or even did I forget the other wheel? Who cares? And then you fall. Every one falls. The living gods of Unicycling fall.

The money does not matter. Your network South Block Washington, Whitehall or Duma does not matter. Your training Marine, Delta Force, SAS, French Legion does not matter. Your country USA, Burkina Faso, Neuve, Cayman or the Outer Hebrides does not matter Your blood group, your cholesterol, your sugar levels, small or large platelet are irrelevant. What key chain you have doesn't matter Harley or Ducati, Rolls, McLaren, Pantera or Donkelvoort. Your address Jurong or Canterbury Road, Malabar or Antop hill, Penthouse or Mansion, Burj Khalifa, Mayfair, Manhattan Central Park... is irrelevant. It is ONLY between you and your Unicycle – always.

Sometime later, I then achieved a tiny molecule of the holy grail: free mount, 50 meters of an unsupported ride and a reasonably okay dismount !!! And then with a mixture of delight and disgust I realised, what has taken me so long and what I am so happy about is just Level 1 of the International unicycling Federation's ten levels! Unicycle, hockey and basketball are too far away.

Unicycling does not differentiate. It does not care what you read.? What is your age or your tastes.? Do you favour Single Malt or Sobranie.? Which food you like, what language you speak, what you listen to, and not even what you like to wear while riding the Unicycle. It treats an

IVY league and Eton and... public, private or government, IIT or IIM equally with disdain. It invites you to try riding it. Yet it does not ask your religion, your food: Kosher, Halal or Jain...

Nothing matters. It is ONLY between you and your Unicycle if you will finally manage to get the hang of it or join the long queue of people who got there and left it.

I was excited. I was happy. I had managed to ride the Unicycle for the first time. I realised it was on a 20-inch unicycle. Unicycles are direct drive so that the speed can be achieved only by increasing wheel size. Mother of GOD, there are 24, 26, 29, 36-inch cycles. And each has different handling and physics; it is like learning all over again!

There are types and types of Unicycling: Trails, street, Mountain Unicycling (I kid you not), Unicycle Hockey and Basketball. Me? I am strictly a distance rider. Even the Unicycle itself; cheapo mass-market or top-of-the-line Kris Holm is irrelevant. Brakes, big or small wheels, cranks and Titanium parts, knobby and plain tires, Carbon fibre, gears or whatever is of no consequence.

There is one wheel, one seat, one rider. All that matters is whether you can roll together. **It Is Only Between You And Your Unicycle – And It Will Always Be That Way.**

. . . .

So after many years of unicycling, I have seven unicycles. Three 20's, one 24, one 26.5 and the king of them all – a 36 inch Coker. I love them all and ride them every day.

It is now just between me and my unicycles, and we have made peace.

. . . .

My zeal to Unicycle has paid me back and how. Believe it or not, I am richer in knowledge with the Unicycling experience. I teach Brand Management, Financial Inclusion and extreme core-fitness with the Unicycle as the centrepiece. To convey the subject in a tactile, haptic proprioceptive way that mere talk, presentations, texts or case studies cannot.

Of late while I unicycle, I think! I begin to wonder how it has been a single refrain, 'It is between the Unicycle and You'.

What if I was to replace the word UNICYCLE and put in anything else !!!!! Say writing, or woodworking, or fear of heights, or relationships… The adrenaline is up again….see you later…and bash on regardless…

. . . .

Miracles, they do happen

Newly married, we were on a long-distance motorcycle ride. It was on a super lonely, long stretch when suddenly I heard the dreaded sound of air escaping - I had a puncture. I had no puncture kit and no foot pump.

The bike was loaded with luggage for a fishing/camping trip and too heavy to push. No idea where the nearest help was. Stupid situation. New motorcycle, newer wife. Cannot leave either for help. It was like the story with a tiger, a goat, a boat, a river and a bundle of grass. And it is getting dark.

Wife has a brilliant idea. 'How about we load the whole rig on top of a truck?' I patiently explain. It would require a miracle of seven components: One empty truck, going in our direction, on a God-forsaken road, at least twenty people on board, willing to help, driver willing to take us and not charge a bomb.

I turned around after smirking at dim women and saw, a yellow PWD truck, full of labourers on their way from a worksite. They stopped for us, lifted the whole rig, dropped us at a puncture shop, did not charge anything and besides treated us to *chai*.

I now expect miracles routinely. Also, since that day, I have never argued with my wife!!

For Your Eyes Only

Ankur Mittal

In the late eighties and early nineties, when I started working, in India, there were a handful of car models to choose from, and few cars on the road. An air-conditioner (AC) in a car, though not unavailable, was a rarity. Even rare was the AC's ability to cool the car. After all, a car was a means to an end. It served the purpose of transporting you from Point A to Point B. Its reason for existence was not to make you comfortable in an AC environment while transporting you, or to ensconce you in a cocoon while shutting out the external sounds, or to enable you to watch your favourite Netflix programme while travelling, as seems to be the case today. At that time, it was a big deal for a person to have a car with an AC.

It was my first job. As it was for several others, who had joined that company as Management Trainees. And we were like sponges. For information. For nuggets dropped by seniors from time to time. Eager to learn and make our way up in life.

One of our many early management lessons was from a senior colleague, who had a Sales job in the company and who believed that it was important to keep up appearances. He, as the concluding lines in a soliloquy on the sexiness of a Sales job, once told us, "It does not matter that you don't have an AC in your car, you should still drive with your windows rolled up. After all, you know you don't have an AC, but the guy outside your car does not. Hence, when someone outside sees you in a car with the windows rolled up, he will naturally think you are travelling in an AC car, and your position in his eyes will grow manifold."

That simple lesson opened our eyes and stayed with us. Landing a job in Sales became a priority. Of course, as in life, so in business; some are more eager than others. One of my Management Trainee colleagues, let us call him Anand, was one such person. A couple of years older than the others. He had worked for two years before joining the MBA programme from where he was hired, the joy at now working for a well-known multinational was writ large on his face. I suspect he had that self-satisfied grin on his face even while he slept. On most days he was the first one to reach office and the last one out. He took to heart all that our seniors told us. He internalised the messages so that he could follow them in all spheres of life, and made sincere efforts to implement them in his work-related affairs. Even telling other naysayers, like me, to start treating the job seriously.

In due course, he was successful in landing a job in Sales. As was I, though, to twist a phrase, not for trying. He spent many joyful road-trips inside his recently purchased Maruti 800 car with windows rolled-up, in the heat and humidity of Kolkata (then Calcutta), feverishly wiping the sweat off his brow and everywhere else his hand could reach. He was happy that his stock, and mine by association, on the few occasions I happened to accompany him, was rising in the eyes of the people outside the car, who of course, he did not know from Adam. But alas! Those joyful days of striving to steadily rise in the eyes of the world came to an end as soon as he got a car with an AC. After all, no more was there a need to paint a picture for the outsider. He actually had a car with an AC. He was downcast for weeks after he got a car with an AC.

It seems like a long time back, when Blackberry handsets had started becoming popular, and one could do emails "on the go". It was fascinating to watch senior people carry them around. They would keep peering into them or typing on their Blackberry, especially when they were inside the elevator, or in a restaurant, or generally in a crowded place. It imbued them with an air of importance. One could almost see the halo around their head. At least they must have felt important. Of course, as relative newcomers, me and my Management Trainee colleagues, though no longer Management Trainees, were not important enough for the company to trust us with one. Neither could we afford one on our own.

It seems, for Anand, our early days' lesson came back to him. He heard the prophetic words again. This time they had morphed to "After all, you know that you don't have a Blackberry handset, but the guy receiving your mail does not." And he sent the next email from his PC with "sent from my Blackberry handset" as the last line.

After that, whenever he sent an email from his PC, it seems he made it a point to type at the bottom "sent from my Blackberry handset". So much so that it became a part of his email signature. Not sure if anyone ever noticed that he sent emails only from his Blackberry handset. He was sure his stock would rise with all the people who received his emails and they would place him in the same category of important people who need to respond to important emails only from their handset even after three days of receipt, especially when they are inside the elevator, or in a restaurant, or generally in a crowded place.

After flirting with the "sent from my Windows Phone" message in his email signature, he finally settled on "sent from my Apple iPhone", the one that he did not have. At some stage, he even updated that line to "sent from my Apple iPhone of the latest model" since Apple kept coming out with new models, and he could not be bothered for updating the message each time a new one came out. He is now covered until eternity. Or, at least till Apple makes phones.

He is constantly window-shopping for newer and more expensive technologies and lifestyle rages that he will never buy. This stuff seems to be addictive. He is hooked onto it.

When he is unable to accept an invite for golf, which we all learned to play while in Kolkata, he always texts saying "Sorry cannot make it. My Honma (one of the more pricey golf equipment brands) set will need to lie in the closet for another week." Of course, if he accepts an invite, he sends out no such message, because of the Honma set that he does not have.

At some stage, he started writing "written by my limited edition Mont Blanc Meisterstuck fountain pen with an 18K hand-ground gold nib with a platinum inlay" on office documents which one might need to still write on. Thankfully a physical signature was still required as proof of authorisation on many documents, else the 'Mont Blanc Meisterstuck fountain pen with an 18K hand-ground gold nib with a platinum inlay,' the one that he did not have, would have needed to lie idle. Each time he signed, it was accompanied by a "signed with my limited edition Mont Blanc Meisterstuck fountain pen with an 18K hand-ground gold nib with a platinum inlay" note just below the signature. He did the same when he signed on the form he had to fill for renewing his Passport. His application got rejected. He was livid. "Seems like the government folks don't get it," was his considered opinion.

Not only that, during meetings in the office, whenever he speaks or needs to concur/ differ, he makes it a point to remind others who the concurrence has been given by. So, if the meeting organisers were to ask at the end of the meeting "do you agree?" if he agreed he would nod his head and follow it up with "this agreement has been given through a shake of the head that could not solve Calculus problems at MIT". If he disagrees, verbally he would say "I disagree" and follow it up with "this disagreement has been voiced by the vocal chords that never spoke out aloud at Oxford." Both factually correct statements, as he never went to either.

In all fairness, Anand made efforts to keep up with the times, as well as the Joneses. And he has acquired a veneer of sophistication. After moving to dry as a bone Gurgaon, which has neither a river, or lake, or canal, or anything that looks remotely like a body of water, except after a short, light drizzle when it closely resembles the Pacific Ocean, with no shore in sight, he made discreet enquiries as to where a yacht the size of a small cruise ship could be parked.

He no longer says, "My superyacht will need to be parked on dry land." People can guess if they want to. Moving from a Blackberry, he did not have to a superyacht he does not have is no mean achievement.

It helps one aspire. It perhaps helps one feel great about what the external world may be thinking about us. But about our self-respect…

We lost touch as he moved on to another city in another job. Last I spoke to him, he sounded like a defeated man, denied the rapid promotions he so coveted, denied the escape from the ordinariness of regular jobs that many of us are engaged in. Before he disconnected the phone, he said, "The world deserves ordinariness. It cannot appreciate people like me."

Har Har Narmada Maa

Srinivas Shastrix

Why would you want to do Ma Narmada Parikrama, when you have already made 9 trips to Ma Narmada in last three years? What is so special about it? And three weeks! Is that the time you are willing and capable to take out? Do you know you are talking of some 2600 KM of travel? Questions I have been asked many times.

The answer was equally simple. It was not that I did because parikrama is the done thing. It is not even as fanciful as Edmond Hillary saying, he climbed Mount Everest because it was there to climb. And the 10th trip if any has to be far more memorable.

It is said that one gets more blessed by just seeing Ma Narmada than even by bathing in Ganga. Ma Narmada is considered as a virgin – always leaping away, which is the reason for Her name Reva ~ The Leaping One. And it is this sacred river, that Ma Ganga also visits to wash away the sins of her devotees.

Narmada, one of oldest rivers of India, flows right through her centre. Emerging from the hills near Amarkantak it flows westward for 1,312 kilometers before meeting the Arabian Sea at Bharuch. Ma Narmada is also known by her various names, few of them are Mekulsuta, Reva, Murla, Samodhbhava, Trikuta, Vanmala, Shoukatmala, Purv-Ganga, Dakshin Ganga, Mahajva, Nandana, Chandana, Gautami, and Mahanand.

I have been hard-pressed to explain Ma Narmada PariCarMa to myself, let alone others A discussion on the eve of the trip with my friend Nish clarified it for me. He was trying to help out Ed Kashi with how to explore his eponymous holy place (Kashi).

The *sArAnsh* (Essence) can only come from within. If you are following the guidance of others, it isn't yours The Master [Sri Ramakrishna] once said that Consciousness was like Water. The bedrock of the Universe is most abundant on Mother Earth. He took me all over various places on Ma Narmada and showed me Her *swarUpa* at Amarkantak. Deep down in the Womb of the Temple at Amarkantak, there She was: looking like Ma Kali.

Do you know, in the Ma Narmada Parikrama, you have to keep Ma Narmada always on your right, and you DON'T cross Ma Narmada during the Parikrama? Well, that was a small condition to comply with. I was determined to do it the way it is prescribed. And so it happened with the grace of Ma Narmada, that I managed to complete the parikrama between 21st November and 12th December 2018.

Such things do need divine intervention. So when Umesh, my IIM-A pal and fellow Basketball player, at Indore was very generous in releasing Ashok Thakur [AshThak] for driving me the entire trip, I saw it as the final green signal, with Shotgun Shastrix becoming the Navigator

AshThak was known to me. I have in past done trips to Nemawar, Hoshangabad, and Omkareshwar with him. I love his spirit and stories; he's a fiery saint, from what I have seen; just a matter of time before his *swarUpa* [real nature] comes out

Then, I opened the trip to others who were interested in joining for a couple of days to a week. The response was unimaginable. It was more than what I anticipated.

The trip needed momentum. Grass (Raj from our gated community) ensured that I didn't have to travel alone. He kicked in on Mon 19th Nov 2018 from Hyderabad, where I went with Srini (who drove me around earlier in 2005) on Sun 18th Nov, and stayed for the entire week till Sun 25th Nov. I am indebted to them for giving the initial momentum.

But, before the trip, one has to plan and get the right gear. The car was already there and the driver released by Umesh. And once again, things seem to fall into place. The Ricoh Theta 360° camera [a cool ₹35K] that VisGupta (from our gated community) so graciously loaned me. My Dell Chromebook. My backup phone with Jio; it would have been impossible to upload the many pics without it. It worked beautifully and only at Amarkantak did its speed falter. The bag from Bob (another batchmate from IIMA) at the National School of Smart Government (NISG) that was so convenient for all my many gadgets. People who know me know that I am a person who travels with more clothes than I need.

The three-week journey has many episodes and incidents that were part of the whole experience. I learned that one must Take the good with the bad. It is essential to keep flowing; don't get stuck at obstacles, flow around them like Lord Krishna, keeping your cool. The main idea is to reach the Great Ocean. Don't pay heed to the machinations of the mind: irrespective of the good stuff that happens, it tends to pick on the missed opportunities and keeps nettling you; look on it as a third party out to irritate you (thanks much to Srinu for this excellent observation)

There were mini-episodes of joy and experience everywhere.

AshThak and Self climbed up to Bhadra Kali Mandir, midway to Mahakali Mandir, but on a separate hill. What a sweeping sight, with the wind howling and threatening to blow off everything not adequately anchored, including my spectacles [have to remove them to read my mobile]

A smart dark girl kid, preening in a green dress, was ahead of me in Bhadra Kali Mandir. She looked up and smiled so benignly and divinely that she enshrined herself in my heart for all time to come. What innocence and a smile of no expectations.

Maheshwar, I find as the prettiest place on Ma Narmada and, for some, the Center of the Universe, which feeling I share. It has always been a terrific experience for me, every time to be on the riverfront. Small joys of life. Late evening, I was fortunate to have the cam and the chance to spend some time sitting with feet in Ma Narmada with a zillion fishes swimming joyfully along the Ghat at Maheshwar and the occasional nibble. Great to see AshThak feeding them *muri* and creating quite a splash. Every time, something new, which is the playful aspect of The Great River Ma Narmada. I know she blesses me.

The Narmada is a Sanskrit word meaning "the Giver of Pleasure". Trust me that is what I experienced in abundance, sitting in front of this majestic River at Narmada Retreat over breakfast at Maheshwar — watching the resplendent ripples on the bosom of The River and birds flying in formation or winging it alone. Leaves were falling off trees and spiraling down for a very long time; the butterfly flitting over the fence, caring two hoots to human-made boundaries, with only the boats breaking the silence, ferrying passengers to Sahastra Dhara falls downstream. How beautiful is that feeling? Maybe that is what I was seeking in a few places and got it here — the inner peace.

Let me share a straightforward incident. It was at Bagdi Sangam, Narmada Madhya Bindyu, Neemwar. We were at the Bhairav Tekri aka Bagdi Sangam Ashram. There as soon as we entered, we ran into a Swami. Frankly, I am not so much into these guys, but he was a very inspiring soul, and we sat and listened to him:

Swamijee used the allusion that I have liked for a long time: the water drops evaporate from the Ocean because they are trying to find their way back, sometimes enjoying their time in ponds and lakes far too long.

Add an interesting observation. Some drops evaporate and fall back soon on the Ocean without seeing land, somewhat like the Isvarkotti such as Swami Vivekananda who accompany avatars like Sri Ramakrishna.

The Swami made my day, And I remembered not to let the self-imposed stereotypes to block your view and way. There can never be any generalisation, and there should not be. God has been so truthfully filling us with untemplated nature, so why should we be categorising and not getting out? In an inclusive world one does not need to overcome biases, because they don't exist.

The day had more in store. We went down to the edge of the river, and I started taking a 360° View. Kids playing at the rived bed were intrigued with what I was doing. I was happy to oblige. And then I wondered how curiosity plays a role. Here were these kids (like other Indians) getting an "experience without the experience"; by seeing someone doing something. In a way, whatever may be the observation and explanation, it does in some ways expand their horizon of worlds view. When Mercedes-Benz tried to foist old models on us in India, we rejected them outright, only due to this "experience without the experience" that we are already exposed to.

Unni & I later at the Bagdi river kept discussing; how we go through childhood, get stuck into the rat race, and a few of us are fortunate to become kids all over; the shorter the Rat Race, the better for you. And that's is my humble opinion.

And as Swamijee has been persistent, we had a light lunch with him. There I met a lady who had done the actual Parikrama twice! And here I was on my first gathering experiences. Folks wear their achievements lightly in these parts. The more they are rooted, the more they are humble about their accomplishments and take it as a part of life.

. . . .

While we are on this experience, I share "my way of looking at the world model", something that I now believe in. My model is a superstructure.

The world is not really real

There's something in the background. Call it Love, Truth, Allah, Brahman, Christ Consciousness, Formless, Self, Wakan Tanka, whatever.

This something is in our (spiritual) hearts as well and is our prime-mover and animator. It's the One that's giving rise to our thoughts, actions, etc.

This Self, which is "out there" as Awareness as well as "in here" as Consciousness, is recording everything. It's a witness to phenomena.

Due to this background Self, we are all connected.

The Universe is an appearance in this Self. It is like a majestic and mysterious dream of the Self.

....

Whatever is possible, I do for the joy of it. If there isn't any, I cut it out of my life. Joy is paramount. That was the main reason for making this trip: to see The River in all her majesty. Got around to knowing some folks even more

The Universe is an appearance in the Self, and it's basically a 3D movie, majestic and mysterious

So no point in getting into a tizzy over the happenings in a game; Nothing Ever Happened

When Ramana Sadguru was asked which theory most gelled with His own experience, he said that it was Ajata (not created). There is no creation, no destruction, no bondage, no longing to be freed from bondage, no striving to be free [from bondage], nor anyone who has attained [freedom from bondage]. Know that this is the ultimate truth.

A Rat Encounter With Cat

S M Sundaram

16th December 1984

Common Admission Test for IIMs

Life wasn't easy as an 18-year old. I was busy doing my CA articleship during the day and pursuing a Bachelor's degree in Commerce in the evenings.

Having lived most of my teen life in the small town of Coimbatore, I had no idea of that an MBA was, let alone what an IIM was. Sometime around October 1984, while staying in a college hostel in Chennai (then, Madras), I saw many of my friends preparing for some test or exam.

It seemed everyone was together in it. It intrigued me as if I was missing out on something important. I asked them what they were up to. The answer what I got was not something that enlightened me. They said they were preparing to appear for CAT. I asked, "What's CAT?" Someone said it is for admission to one of the IIMs. Next question, "What's IIM?" And thus, the conversation event along.

Blissfully unaware of what this was all about, I continued with my focus on my CA articleship and the important intermediate exams that would come up in less than a year. That less than 1% passed this exam only made me redouble my efforts in preparing for it. With the articleship involving full-time work from 9 am to 5 pm, followed by evening college from

5.30 to 8.30 pm, I hardly had time to think about something called MBA, which I understood nothing about.

However, with the humdrum of CAT preparations going on around me in the hostel, it was difficult to contain my curiosity. What was this CAT all about?

Looking around, I wondered 'if these guys could write this exam CAT or whatever it was, maybe I could too'. So, two days before the deadline for the applications expired, I bought the CAT application form; it cost me Rs. 10 and applying to three of the IIMs left me poorer by Rs. 30 each! Even this event had its own set of drama. I was out of town on audits and had to rely on an unreliable office assistant to mail the applications. He did remember to do it, but only just!

After the applications were gone, the equivalent of buyer's remorse hit me. Had I wasted the considerable sum of one hundred rupees on something I knew nothing about? A hundred rupees was a princely sum in the mid-1980s.

D-day arrived. 16th December 1984. On the morning of this fateful day, I took out the 'Hall ticket', which had unambiguous instructions on it. And the very first instruction right at the top read 'Bring a pen, pencil, eraser and sharpener'.

Pencil? Eraser? Sharpener? What are all these for? Am I a school kid or what? "Bah!" I smirked.

I landed at the exam centre at Stella Maris College, Madras with an old Reynolds ballpoint pen's chewed out blue cap sticking out of my shirt pocket. Some of my hostel mates who travelled with me to the centre had the full paraphernalia – including the pencil, eraser and sharpener. I smirked at them silently – kids!!

10 minutes before the scheduled start...

The exam hall doors were thrown open. There were rows of long tables, where candidates were seated at double arm's length from each other. I settled into my allotted seat and looked around. Everyone was busy laying out their pens, pencils, erasers and sharpeners on the table. I smirked and rolled my eyes yet again. Kids!!

5 minutes before the scheduled start…

The answer/response sheets for MCQ (multiple choice questions) were distributed. I glanced at the list of instructions. The smirk vaporized in nanoseconds. My gaze refused to go past instruction no. 1: Mark all your answers in pencil!

I looked around once again at all the pencils, erasers and sharpeners in front of each person. All except me, of course! And suddenly, my eyes widened! The boy with thick glasses at the other end of my long table had two pencils! TWO lovely, shining, brand new pencils with immaculately (and probably lovingly) manicured and sharpened tips!!

Flashing at him what I thought was a charming smile, which in reality may have been an embarrassed and sheepish grin, I asked him "Can you please lend me a pencil?"

His response was as short as it was to the point (pun not intended): "No"!

3 minutes before the scheduled start…

Not knowing what to do, I just sat there. The only thing I remember was that I was just cool as a cucumber. Not flustered. No butterflies in the stomach. No panic. Just a matter-of-fact acceptance of the situation.

I guess not knowing what an IIM means does have its benefits!

1 minute before the scheduled start…

"Here", I heard. I turned towards the voice. The same boy who said "No" was handing over one of his precious pencils to me! No thank you had ever sounded more sincere – not before and not since.

CAT started…

Pencil furiously blackening out empty circles as I raced through the sections. 70 questions in 15 minutes in English. 70 questions in 35 minutes in Mathematics… and so on.

Inevitably, I goofed up on some of the responses. My moist fingertips became my eraser. When they weren't moist enough, the tip of my tongue made sure they were! The invigilator, a sweet lady in her mid-thirties with those eyes that are waiting for someone to try something fresh, was looking at me with an initial disinterest which slowly transformed to curiosity.

She saw me trying to erase the wrong answers with my moist fingers, occasionally wetting them with the tip of my tongue. Coming over, she whispered to me "Don't do that; they may deduct points for neatness" and quietly handed over an eraser that she had borrowed from another student. Words stuck in my throat. I couldn't even whisper my gratitude to her. I guess my eyes said it all.

Over the remainder of the exam, every single time I needed an eraser, she would patiently and indulgently get me one and then take it back to the owner. Not once, not twice, not thrice, but over a couple of dozen times over the two hour exam. Not to forget a couple of instances when I needed a pencil sharpener as well.

Fast forward to March 1985…

Group Discussion… check.

Interview… check. Instructions were followed to the letter, needless to say.

30th April 1985, as the final semester exams approached, came the letter on the IIM Ahmedabad letterhead which read: "Dear Mr Sundaram. I am glad to inform you that you have been selected for provisional admission to IIMA's Post-Graduate Programme in Management for the session beginning 2nd July 1985…"

Whew!

....

Innumerable times over my life, I have thought of that fateful day. Two strangers sculpted what was inarguably the most pivotal day of my life. To this day, I know not who they are. I wish I did. I hope they read this and something flickers in their memory enough for them to say "Hey! That was me!" Till then, all I can do is to continue to pay their generosity forward. And continue to thank them and pray that they reaped the karma for transforming someone's life that day immeasurably.

And that too, from the bottom of my socks, because the bottom of my heart is not deep enough!

....

Strategy or Destiny!

Rajeev Kakar

I wanted to be a Robotics researcher. No, I wanted to be an entrepreneur. No, I wanted to run a factory – and be like that Hindi Film industrialist have 'Kakar Group of Industries'

I am now a global financial service professional. You can call me a banker. And that pretty much sums up my life. It was as if, the moment I made a plan, someone up there decided, let's change it for Rajeev

A quick look at my story will substantiate what I have to say later.

I was and in some ways still am, an engineer at heart. Numbers, precision, and certainty define my approach to life. I wove those approaches from my subjects in Engineering. I was admitted to the PhD program in robotics at Rochester, fully funded by a much-needed scholarship and was waiting for the completion of formalities to hit the USA. There was some I20 document we were waiting for. They were delayed owing to snail mail.

It was at this time, that I decided to take the IIM, Ahmedabad call as insurance. Everyone knew that IIMA was the BEST in India made business institutes, and it was hard for me to risk losing it, just in case my I20 did not come. However, I was so sure, it was an experiment and that the I20 would come that I had even booked my return ticket to Delhi where my

parents lived. It was slated for 20 days after the course started...
intending to leave for the world of Robotics at Rochester.

As an IIT engineer, I was trained to make decisions using
every element of data available, analyzing them collectively
with precision, and without ignoring a single data item...but
the IIM, Ahmedabad management approach shocked me. It
was asking me to start learning how to discard most data. The
engineer in me wondered how numbers can ever be unwanted?
It was forcing me to eliminate so-called noise, and instead
focus on the two or three critical drivers, to find 'optimal'
solutions. It was about un-learning five years of IIT learning to
find solutions that met 'precision'!.

I began to adjust to my new normal of working under
uncertainty!!! Accounting really got my goat. I was shocked to
learn that Assets (usually a term for something 'that is sought'!)
were to be classified as DEBITS and Liabilities (typically
referring to something 'unwanted'!) as CREDITS! I thought
this management world is crazy.

So, I used my ticket to get as far as possible from Vastrapur
and got back to Delhi! I was suddenly put off by the prospect
of studying further. I felt it was mindless, to now make me start
unlearning everything that had first taken me five years of hard
work to learn. One crazy world, this was!

A series of things happened over the next seven days. Slow
U.S. universities, snail mail, well-wishers, mentors, pressure
from my parents to return to academics, and the retreat of my
obstinacy- all had a role to play. It resulted in me getting back
to Ahmedabad' kicking and screaming', to do the management
course at IIM. The next two years were fantastic fun-filled
years, and graduating near the very top of my class.

*I must say, I had the advantage of having my own advisory
board which helped me in making the decisions. In fact, each of*

us must have one. They might be parents, well-wishers, friends, mentors or whoever.

There will be times when like me, you will be unable to make a decision, and such a 'Board' can help catalyze thinking and clarify situations. And a well-chosen board can insulate you from your hubris, youthful arrogance and of course obstinacy. It cannot stress more. Over time I too grew and matured to become my own trusted advisor. And maybe good enough to play that role for someone else!

Came graduation, I chose not to participate in campus placement. Instead, I returned to Delhi to set up a factory (Dad gifted me an industrial plot of land) and become an entrepreneur like my father.

Destiny played a part yet again! I happened to go along with an IIMA classmate to collect his appointment letter from American Express. The H.R. manager, apparently in the business of recruiting trespassers, strangely gave me one too! And I took it!

My motivation to join American Express was to be based in Delhi, continue working towards starting my factory and only to make a coveted trip overseas as a perk. I hated my job and, in ten months after my first overseas travel, to Hong Kong, I quit. But again, not to start my factory.

This time destiny had me enticed by Citibank, and I was promptly dispatched to the only Indian city I did not wish to go to, i.e. Kolkata.

Once in Kolkata, I sort of fell in love with the place and wanted to stay on. But, soon the bank sent me to Delhi, and then in a couple of years to Mumbai. And in two years to Chennai, and then again to Delhi where I got my first big break. I took charge of my first CEO role at the young age of 32 and founded a J.V. Auto finance company between Citi and Maruti, and ran it as the Founder MD & CEO.

I was on a roll, and the factory plans kept getting postponed, but I did make my dream of becoming an entrepreneur within the bank.

Soon, as a typical Citibanker, I started aspiring for international assignment and posting. I wanted to go overseas and work in global markets, anywhere was acceptable but not in the continent of Africa. But destiny had it defined for me yet again, and Citi sent me to Egypt, precisely the place in the world I did not want to be in.

It is different that, once in Egypt, I fell in love with the place. I established Citi's new operations and broke-even the business in record time! And then just as my family and I were beginning to enjoy the Cairo lifestyle, the bank sent me to Turkey.

I wondered! Was I not supposed to be 'star'. Why they send me to Turkey....where no Citibanker has ever succeeded in over nine years, amidst the characteristic Turkish volatility and hyper-inflation environment. If everyone had failed there, why/how would I survive was the question on my mind! Why me? Once again, I resisted in my characteristic style! But soon I found myself transported to the mystical and beautiful city of Istanbul.

Once again, we were unsure about coming in, and it turned into a deep love for this paradise city. I successfully turned-around the business, recovering cumulative past nine-year of losses over the next two years!

No point in guessing my reward for success. The bank, instead of letting me bask in comfort with my family in the delightful land of Turkey, moved me to Dubai! This time, it was layered with a promotion to head the entire 'Turkey, Middle East, and Africa' region! Damn.....it was upsetting and, indeed, unsettling for the kids and us.

Why could I not be allowed to manage the region from Istanbul? However, I soon found where all this was leading to. The GREAT BIG team in the sky was working overtime. It was uprooting me every two-three years, moving me around like a pawn, albeit to a more significant and more substantial role each time. Damm it, We had in just two decades at Citibank and moved 11 cities across countries.

When we were looking at the UAE as a market, the BRICS classification was very popular, especially in the emerging markets context. The UAE was seen as a very 'dispersed' market with very little financial inclusion.

When I took another hard look at the market, I found there was another way to classify/segment the market. When you peel away the primary higher-income layers, you find a substantial middle/ lower income layer. It looks exactly like emerging markets: the same type of demographics, aspirations and ethnicities! In other words, while the aggregate gave one picture; numbers, precision, and open-mindedness revealed a totally different picture.

So, somewhere the IIMA learning came back. While learning is important, "unlearning and relearning" in a hurry is just as important. This is all the more so when venturing into uncharted territory-unknown markets.

No case study or textbook is available to tell you what to do when you hit a new market like Rwanda, or Mongolia...it is all up to how quick you are in sizing up the action. You just **Dig Deep and Hard – and unlearn.**

And then, in 2006, after two years in Dubai, I was moved to Citi London, and destiny played its part again. Around the same time, I was headhunted by Temasek to be one of the five global CoFounders of Fullerton Financial Holdings. The mandate - to create and operate banks in various Emerging markets globally.

The choice was between moving to London with Citi (the biggest market cap company at the time) or to Singapore to create Fullerton Global (a Zero market cap company at that point of inception).

I negotiated with both to be allowed to live on in Dubai and do either of the roles – both global and involving extensive travel. Temasek won, as they agreed to base me out of Dubai. This meant, my family stayed in Dubai and I, in a plane. I reluctantly took the chance!

There are often, times when one refuses to shift location due to family constraints, usually to do with children's education. I have found it to be the other way around. Our family moving to over 11 locations in 20 years, proved to be a huge asset. Apart from professional exposure for me, children grew up to be true global citizens. They got the authentic, first-hand experience of what it is like to live in India, Turkey, Egypt, UAE, or the USA – first, second, third worlds. It has been of immense help in their being able to get college admissions in the finest schools in the U.S. and be prepared to fit-in and live or work anywhere in the globe.

I regretted it soon after. There was nothing but a plain canvas to start with. Meanwhile, my alma mater Citi's stock price was at its peak, and when I joined Fullerton, I was forced to sell out. At that time, there was an expectation for the stock to double over the next 3-5 years. Damn….why did I have to do it!

God was at play again with my career!

However, just like in the past, destiny had it all worked out for me strangely! Come 2008, the Great Financial Crises rocked the world. I was saved. The Citi stock crashed. In the interim in Fullerton, we successfully started creating new banking franchise across the globe.

So what made me do it? Not money, money can wait and will finally come. I believe in learning before you seek to earn! For me, it has always been to decide the criteria to choose paths. If the path is new and offers me learning, I have always jumped for it. My reasons were manifold, including the thing about being based out of Dubai, but more important were the chance to innovate, be noticed and most importantly prepare continuously for these changing times.

Over the next 13 years, Fullerton created history while the mighty crumbled. I travelled end-to-end. Indonesia to China to Russia to Mexico… Name an emerging market, and I have gone there, creating, acquiring, transforming new banks and financial institutions in 12+ countries, and soon building value of over USD 40Bn in size. And in process clocking 6 million airline miles over 10 years! I even founded 'Dunia Finance' a greenfield Finance company locally in the UAE, since the home was in Dubai. With a positive mindset, it was possible to find new opportunity everywhere.

So much for strategy, and kudos to destiny! All happenstance!

One thing I clearly understand, the Business deal with Cultural Acclimatization,. And it is not the other way around. Places like USA, U.K., UAE, Egypt, Turkey, Qatar, Saudi Arabia, Oman, India, Pakistan, Israel, wait there is a reason for this list, Vietnam, Indonesia, Singapore, Malaysia, Cambodia, China, Russia, Mexico……are where I sometimes lived, sometimes visited, sometimes did business in. And here's the thing, if you have a working business deal, the cultural stuff is just icing.

One is taught that in Japan, you must bow, in Greece, you should not use the Mountza gesture; in Thailand, don't show your feet. All very nice. But these do not make business deals happen. First and foremost get your business deal in place. Be polite and globally well mannered. The rest is just icing on the cake.

In the countries I worked, I have had staff: bosses, colleagues, and subordinates coming from across the world. It took time, but I realized and then ensured that I was not using my stereotypes. It helped me in working with people irrespective of their religion, colour, language, culture, gender and customs. In a way, it helped me be a global citizen.

Its importance is further accentuated, as we grow ever more connected. I have realized as I shed my stereotypes, I begin to appreciate people. I started beginning to fall in love with their cultures, foods, cities and way of life, in every town I lived in. Being able to survive, no thrive, amongst different languages, cuisines and working styles is a huge advantage in a globally connected economy.

There has been quite a lot of madness in my career. There was planned chaos and unpredictability. But, there was a set of learning which made me what I am today. However, in the interests of numbers, precision, and certainty; please remember, these are only general directions and the choices I made within them. Indeed you must generate your own flavours. And make your peace with whatever game the universe plays with you.

And the final thing, there is something called, '**Being in the Right Place at the right time**'. This is a cliché, but like most clichés, it is absolutely true. I fully endorse it. I got into the auto finance business in CITI just as the auto industry in India took off, and it was a breathtaking success. It happened in Egypt, and then in each of my different moves across cities, countries, and even companies.

I was lucky to be in the right place at the right time. But the engineer in me twists this cliché with more precision to work in my favour. You improve your odds of being in the right place at the right time if you are in more places at more times. And that's precisely what I mean by saying choose the paths that are new and offer new learning. That way you hedge your bets.

I have been fortunate. And I can vouch for the impact of giving it back. It is crucial to 'LEARN, EARN, and RETURN" to country, society, family…whatever. For moral, ethical and philosophical reasons… also because it is uplifting in a spiritual sense. However, I have a personal philosophy: giving back has to be firmly linked to my skills, knowledge and expertise. To this end, I have chosen two major thrust areas: Financial Inclusion and Art. The first is abundantly clear: financial inclusion for all is the banker's dream. Art needs a little more thinking. For very long, art has seen finance or even money in general as evil. And if you canvass art (even bankers are permitted puns!), you find something startling. Viewer evaluates art aesthetically, on its promise, longevity or monetarily. This is absolutely the same as all financial products. At a deep level, I believe art and financial products are synonymous. I now wish to introduce art and artists to the complex world of finance and vice versa. Who knows, I may become an artist of sorts myself.

So do plan for giving back. It will make the long haul that much more rewarding.

Now, you know me a bit. If I sift through my experience, it will lead me to one inescapable, almost mathematical conclusion: strategy and planning are not all. Deep breathing please, I am not taking away your jobs or making you doubt your management degree! Hang on, while I explain.

Strategy and planning will generate yields only when executed, delivered, harvested and cycled back with negative feedback (apologies, I am an engineer) to strengthen and stabilize the system. The easiest of these is the planning, excel sheet, PERT chart or whatever. There are so many uncertainties, especially with the global economic situation being so volatile. With digitally enabled financial markets the idea of strategic planning seems purely academic. In an ivory tower. Supremely isolated as well.

Ask me. I would say execute, execute, execute, survive, thrive and somewhere along you will see the whole thing coalesce into a strategy. This I have seen, experienced and I believe... Hell from Points A to Z above, that's what I have been doing for you. Execution to strategy, not the other way around!!

....

And now for a couple of personal takeaways, you may call it gyan, but then I have gone through the hardship to serve it to you on a platter.

TIME is your only resource. And if as a max banker I am saying time is money, it is because I mean it. I am not presumptuous. I have empirical evidence. In 32 years what I have been able to achieve, is only because I invest (not spend) time with demonic obsession. Every second of it. Time REALLY is money. I won't say more, because I do not have the time to do it !!!

HOME is where you are. As a global manager, where you are is home. There is no going back anywhere 'home'. If you can achieve this mindset, you've hit a HOME RUN!

Good luck and Godspeed in whatever you do. And if something that you read here works for you, just give something back to society. You can reach me at rajeevkakar@yahoo.com, but only if there is a relevant discussion, thought or proposal. You know, time is the only resource.

SECTION-C
Interaction

The Write Way

Chiranjeev Kohli

We called him the Godfather. It was a name I had come up with, and it was an apt one. He was authoritative and intimidating, and unsurprisingly, he was feared. He was my Ph.D. advisor, Dr John Summers, who spent most of his career in the Marketing Department of the Indiana University School of Business, and was considered one of the best academic researchers in marketing.

According to some academic papers we discussed during his Methodology Seminar, there are five sources of power. Legitimate power; based on the position or role in the organization. Reward power; the ability to offer rewards or compensation. Coercive power; the ability to punish. Referent power; the ability to influence others who have some control over you. And Expert power; because of knowledge and expertise. And which did he have over me? All five! But not all of them were the source of my fear.

I already knew that he was neither mean spirited, nor one to play favourites. He was a family man with solid values—and his doctoral students were treated like an extended family. In fact, his doctoral seminar was not held on campus like a conventional class, but in the basement of his home. We sat around a large table and discussed the papers till late at night over post-dinner snacks. He took pride in the work his doctoral students did with him and the success they subsequently had in their careers in universities around the country.

But before you could step into that circle, you had to clear a threshold of dedication. As he mentioned in my phone call with him in late 2019, "I didn't want to work with anyone not willing to work hard, because I would be miserable and they would be miserable." He regularly used to quote how he and one of his previous doctoral students responded to a reviewer's comments with—get this—eighty-two single-spaced pages. (Yes, I still remember that number after 30 years). Just so that you know, a typical academic paper is 15 single-spaced pages; and this was just their reply to the critique someone had in the double-blind peer-review process. That's the work ethic he prided himself with.

So, why did he strike fear among doctoral students? For me, it was something akin to expert power. And, that too, not because he was going to use it against me. My source of fear was inside me—of not living up to his demanding expectations. I respected him for that, and I was not ready to let him or myself down. I was ready to learn from him whatever I could. And, yes, we all learned a lot. That he gave us a sound grounding in methodology is not surprising; that came with the territory. From my experience working with Dr Summers, the most important learning is not in my dissertation, but instead, in how my dissertation came about—especially from the meeting we had after he agreed to work with me.

As most doctoral students do, I spent a couple of months searching for a topic which interested me, and where I felt I could make a contribution. Once I had that, I spent another few weeks deliberating on the topic and mentally outlining my work. Then, excited about what I had to share, I walked into Dr Summers' office. "So, what do you have for me?" he asked.

I eagerly began to detail my proposed topic. But I didn't get too far. I was interrupted by, "Can you show it to me?" "I don't have anything written, but it's all laid out in my head," I replied. "Unless you have it written down, it means nothing."

"Unless it's on paper, you have nothing." His words made me freeze in my shoes. I was so excited about my brilliant idea, and this is the response I get? I felt disappointed and irritated. But I knew better than to express my frustration. Instead, I told him I would come back once I had something written down—just as he wanted. And I walked out of his office.

This was not an a-ha moment for me. For that matter, I had not bought into his mantra. I had conducted myself long enough without writing things down and felt I could continue to do so.

Back in my own office, as promised, I started jotting down my thoughts. As they became clearer, the writing also started showing signs of less than stellar logic and a disjointed flow in my thinking. The more I wrote, the better I got at making connections and seeing where I needed to improve. And as these flaws surfaced, it dawned on me that a lot more drafts were needed before I could really believe that what I had was worth sharing. That's how the process started, …and continues to this day. If it is anything worthy, it has to be written down. If clarity is needed, it has to be written down. If a debate of ideas or arguments is needed, it has to be written down. This is something I have taken to heart—for a good reason. Writing your thoughts concretizes them.

I have used this for my own plans, and with my clients, my children, and my wife. No, really. Let me just share a couple of lines on each, so you can also have an appreciation for it.

I did a fair amount of consulting in branding—specifically brand identity. The problem is that it is somewhat abstract, and everyone believes they are an expert. Ask them to write two lines of programming code, and most throw up their arms. Mention branding and everyone has an opinion because it is not a mathematical theory or an axiom that can be proven or disproven. For my first couple of assignments, I fumbled. After doing what I felt was extensive preparation, and presenting my "solutions," I was told that it was not in line with their brief. That's when I realized there was a dissonance between what my clients felt they were conveying, and what I was understanding. Not only did I need to have clear thinking to meet their briefs, I needed my clients to clearly articulate their needs. During the conversations, they were listing ten-plus things they wanted a one or two-word brand name to capture—an unrealistic task. I wanted them to be specific, but they were all over the place. So, I created a two-page form with questions they had to answer—in writing. And it worked. It helped them be more focused and realize that they needed to be precise in what they wanted.

I talked to my children about the importance of hard work and excelling in school. (I had to live up to the stereotype of Indian parents!). When my daughter and son were in middle-school (5th and 7th grade, respectively, if I am not mistaken), I had them write a one-page statement of their goals—and some statements with pre-specified response categories like "I want to be the best," "I want to be average," and "I don't care where I stand." I think I still have those completed forms with me. After writing down their goals, I could see a change in their demeanours and a more focused mindset. The process had emphasized clarity and created a sense of commitment.

Finally, I've used the same strategy with my wife. We argue. I am willing to believe that you don't argue with your spouse, but I have to admit that I argue with mine. Of course, it's never my fault (!). The thing I often noticed was that once we would get started, we would argue on and on until we lost track of what the original point was. So, we agreed—at my insistence—that if it is a major issue, we have to jot it down. We started doing just that. If it is a minor thing, we talk it out; but more problematic concerns have to be written down. It doesn't always work when you are in the heat of an argument. But if one of us has the presence of mind to step out of it, we write down what bothers us and email it. And want to know something funny? I sometimes realize I don't really have anything to fight over. Or, if I do have a beef, it's far less complicated or problematic than I initially believed when thoughts were running amok in my mind.

Try it. Be it a marketing plan or anything else, causing turmoil in your mind, write it down. Writing will bring clarity; and solace.

Being Human

Srikumar

It was 2003. I was with a multinational bank's centralized processing unit at Chennai. This unit was responsible for offshore processing for businesses in a few of the countries.

As in a large multinational, the unit had sub-verticals with some overlapping interests. There was corporate banking vertical, a consumer banking vertical (which I was heading), a software vertical and few more. The bank employed approximately some 3,000 people in these verticals. My unit then had around 700 people.

Now being a senior executive of a relatively standalone unit of the bank, one was often called up to resolve things. More so, there was always that 'Houston, we have a problem' kind of situation. These would have no precedent. Net result, I did not have the classic depend on the experience to address them. All I could rely on was my sense of judgment. Everyone expected you to be mature, understanding, fair and to take charge of the situation.

Now, as there was always a shortage of right talent, as a policy, we often moved skilled employees across verticals. HR had taken this to a new perspective. If someone resigned in any vertical, they would check if some other vertical could accommodate the already verified culturally aligned employee. It made their task simpler.

So, I was not surprised when I got a call from the HR (Human Resource) department. They said someone was resigning and asked if I could meet him. I agreed as I was anyway looking for some talented people and had few suitable vacancies in the vertical.

HR informed me that the person has already resigned on health grounds. The HR wanted to counsel him to stay on. For the next 4-5 days, the head of the employees current vertical was not expected to be in town and hence the request for me to speak with him. I quickly asked the HR representative to bring the person to my office.

Once the HR was clear that I was ready to meet the person, he shared the final bit of information. The employee in question was recently diagnosed with AIDS.

In those days, AIDS was a bomb you never understood. The cause was a matter for speculation, and no cure was in sight. It also had a huge social stigma attached to it. Remember it was 2003.

Now, Yes, the bank, like every other bank, did organize AIDS awareness programs, but that was many months after this incidence.

At that instance, when the HR was dropping the AIDS bomb, all I knew was based on whatever I have read about it. And it was quite limited.

I knew

- AIDS could not spread by breathing the same air or shaking hands
- How AIDS could be transmitted
- It was a societal taboo for the individual and family.

That's where my knowledge ended. I had no idea of the symptoms. I did not know how to interact with an AIDS patient and the sensitivities. Forget about medication and support needed by them.

I had to make a decision. The terrain has been altered. Was I still willing to meet the person? Ducking the meeting was the easy way out, and no one was there to question it. The employee in question was anyway not part of my unit. On the other side, it would be bad for the employee, for the senior executive of the other group, and things can never be hidden forever. How will my team look at me in future, knowing that I refused to meet the employee?

I asked HR to seat the person in an interview room. There were many such rooms on the ground floor. After re-scheduling some internal meetings and getting personally ready for the encounter, I went to meet Ravi (name changed).

When I went to the interview room, I saw that Ravi was seated farthest away from the door. He was alone in the room and visibly terribly stressed. I could sense the awkwardness. He knew that I knew that he had AIDS. He looked at me with a lot of diffidence and greeted me. I went to him, shook his hands and greeted him by the first name. I checked if he had been served tea, which is SOP (standard operating procedure) and is typically done for all interview candidates. To my surprise, the answer was in negative. So, I went out, asked for tea for both of us, and then came back to complete the interview.

I did not know how to conduct a conversation in such a situation. However, I just dived into the case. I enquired about his family situation and his plans. All the time, I was reassuring him. I told him, I knew he had AIDS and I assured him there we were there with him in this situation iind offered a few other soothing words that took just a few minutes of conversation.

Ravi was now a bit relaxed. He wept while speaking of his family. He was burdened with the social trauma in his neighbourhood. There was a silent questioning in every eye contact and stare, be it the shopkeeper or the neighbours or the friends he was having tea with.

It was then that I ventured into real work territory and asked him about his role in the bank, why was he leaving and offered him a similar position in my unit.

He was quite shocked at the offer of a role. He had never imagined that the bank will make any attempt to hold him back. He was preparing to be socially isolated from the bank, and that was the real reason for his resignation.

He promised to rethink. He said he needed time to re-evaluate and try seeing the future that may not be there.

After a few days, he did come back but said he was not staying. He feared and rightly so that the news of his condition will never remain a secret; it is bound to be known. It will inevitably spread, and his colleagues would surely avoid his company.

I tried to convince him. I pointed out that he needed the income. But he had made up his mind. Saab Aap Jaisey Nahi Hote. Everyone is not like you. He said over the phone.

I stayed in touch, but, sadly, he died within a few months of that meeting.

This meeting, which lasted about an hour, has stayed with me.

I distinctly remember the wild expression of shock on his face when I met him, greeted him and shook his hand. He was surprised not because I was from another vertical and a senior; he was surprised because I was shaking his hands after knowing he had AIDS.

There was that expression of utter gratitude on his face. Not because I was offering him an alternate position but because I was interacting with him as I would with any other employee.

When I offered him the alternate position, his eye shouted, 'Is this really true'.

I can't forget the expressions. They are etched in my mind.

Society can be cruel. Just a human touch is sometimes all that is needed to restore someone's self-respect, even if only a little.

Let me be honest. I was not wholly comfortable meeting someone with AIDS. One must remember that it was around 2003; many of us were not adequately aware of AIDS. There was no real fear, but to do what one believed what was right.

Yet, this is not about me at all.

It is about being human. It is about another human. Someone who for all practical purpose knew he was going to die— a person who was getting ready to the possibility and reality of societal intolerance and societal ostracism.

It is about a family. He had to take care of them, and they had to take care of him — basically a decent human just like most of us. Cruel fate had dealt him a bad hand.

It is about someone who made me rise above my insecurities and myself. Ravi, I will remember you with affection and gratitude all my life.

The Visit

Umesh Sharraf

The persistent ring of the doorbell stopped me. I wrapped the thin cotton towel, hanging from a nail by the mirror, around my waist and with the shaving foam obscuring half of my face, went and opened the door and peered out. The Inspector standing outside sucked in his belly, stamped his right foot and brought his right hand up crisply to the peaked cap perched on his head. The salute was so sharp that his palm kept vibrating for an instant. As I looked on fascinated, he barked, "When will my officer be ready?"

"How the hell would I know? Go and ask your officer!" I replied crossly, banged the door shut and returned to the bathroom. The bell buzzed again. I sighed and returned to the door. The Inspector was apologetic, "Sir, I was only asking when my officer will leave the guesthouse?" "I told you, I don't know! Why don't you go and … ask … your … officer, whoever it is!" I said in exasperation. He appeared close to tears at this unreasonable answer and continued to stare at me, quivering in desperation. I shut the door and went back to my toilet.

I put on my uniform and picked up my briefcase; it had papers I had been studying the previous night; and pressed the calling bell to summon the orderly to have the room cleaned up in my absence. As I moved towards the dining room of the guesthouse, I saw the Inspector hovering in the lawn. As I sat down for breakfast, I asked the bearer to call the Inspector inside. He came in and stood expectantly. "Have you found your officer?" I asked. He raised his bushy eyebrows heavenwards in mute supplication. A sudden doubt assailed me. "Are you waiting for me, by any chance?" A smile of pure joy suffused him, and he nodded vigorously and added, "Yes, Sir, I am waiting for my officer only!"

To use of the second person to address an IPS officer was a sacrilege. He could have approached me only in the third, to show due deference and required servility? I sighed, "What do you want?"

"Sir, my SP has sent me to get my officer to my SP's office."

So finally the new Superintendent of Police had found time for me. After the initial training at the National Police Academy, I was now in Kakinada, a coastal town in Andhra Pradesh, the district headquarters of the East Godavari district, for the practical district training of six months. I had been in the government guesthouse for three days. During the time I took to travel to Kakinada from Hyderabad, the SP had been transferred, and the replacement had taken charge. I was yet to meet the new SP who had been busy taking over.

"Welcome to the district. I hope you will apply yourself diligently to the district training and learn practical policing. Many IPS officers fail to learn anything in this period. I will be watching you," the SP warned me, his right hand twirling his moustache. I watched in awe as he teased his magnificent moustache again. He reminded me of a Tamil film hero with his dense hairstyle like a wig and stylish sideburns. He patted and smoothened his hair, already smoothened with copious coconut oil, which I could smell from that distance. He added, "I will draw up your training schedule later. However, today you will proceed to Peddapuram where the Dy.S.P. is expecting you. He is inspecting Tuni police station on my instructions.

You will accompany him and observe how an inspection is carried out. Remember, he is a very experienced police officer and take this opportunity to learn from him." I saluted him and came out where my orderly was waiting with the motorcycle. When I had reported in the district, this jack of all trades had been bestowed on me almost as a dowry with the motorcycle . I told him that we were off to Peddapuram and off we went, I riding pillion.

We rode into the compound of the DSP's office-cum-residence, half an hour later. *The DSP is getting ready. The ASP under-training is requested to kindly be seated.* I looked over the newspaper lying on his table as I waited in the front room, which served as his office. Gods and Goddesses adorned every surface in that room. A large calendar of Lord *Balaji* hung opposite his chair. Photo frames hung on the other three walls had Guru *Nanak*, Mother Mary holding baby Jesus, and the *Kaaba* looking down in divine benevolence. As I was developing regard for the pure, impartial secularism of this police officer, I also espied the picture of Goddess *Laxmi* showering rays of gold coins from her left hand, her right hand raised in blessing, under the glass tabletop. "ASP sahib, *Balaji* is the most powerful God. Have you been to Tirupati yet?" the DSP bustled into the room and lit an incense stick, swirled it before *Balaji* and stuck it in a hole in the wall by the calendar. I expressed my regret. "No. Not yet. But what do you mean by powerful? Are not all gods powerful?"

He looked at me pityingly. "Are all politicians equally powerful? Are all officers equally powerful? How can all gods be equally powerful? Do you know He is the richest God in the world?" I professed my ignorance again. "No matter, no matter. You will learn. You are a child yet. We will teach you." As I wondered about the sudden return of my childhood, he caught me by the hand and dragged me inside. "You must have breakfast." "No, no. I had had breakfast before I started." "Nonsense. You had it in the morning. Now you can have it with me again. The town Inspector has sent hot breakfast." I saw his dining table loaded with *dosas* wrapped in plantain leaves, mounds of white *idlis*, casseroles containing *upma, sambar, rasam* and steel boxes containing coconut, ginger, chili and jaggery *chutneys*, a plate of sticky ghee sweets and two large thermoses of what turned out to be coffee and milk, to which Horlicks had been added. "I am a forced bachelor. My family is in Hyderabad. My meagre food requirements are graciously met by the town inspector," the DSP explained as his town Inspector standing in a corner in the dining room nodded happily at his good fortune in being of some service to his DSP. The DSP munched through his breakfast steadily. "Remember, the police job is full of uncertainty. You never know when you will get your next meal- a good breakfast is very important," he spoke, dribbling *sambar* over his chin which he wiped away with the back of his hand.

After I had the coffee and he the Horlicks laden milk, we adjourned to his office. "Are we going for the Inspection?" He was indulgent, "Yes, of course. We have to give those guys some time to get ready, you know. The SP told me to inspect the PS only in the morning. We can't drop in on the police station unannounced!"

As he dismissed the town Inspector of Peddapuram, I asked my orderly to stay back and got into his jeep with the DSP. On the way to Tuni PS, he patiently elaborated as to how the police station staff was a bunch of crooks everywhere and how these dens of vice could be kept under control only by tight supervision and constant monitoring. He cautioned me that I, a young IPS officer, should not believe a word of these corrupt and lazy rogues. He also stressed how the experience of seasoned hands like him helped the district SP in keeping his head over water...

The jeep halted before Tuni town PS in a cloud of dust. The Sub Inspector came running out, shouting alerts to his constables who were lounging in the small courtyard of the PS. The Tuni Inspector, whose office was in the same building, stumbled out to the road, clutching his cap with one hand and belt with another, hitched up his trousers and shoved his SI aside as both of them saluted. The DSP got down leisurely. "Why were you not waiting on the road?" he bawled at the Inspector and looked at me to show how it was done. We then entered the courtyard that was a few feet deep and a few yards long. A dozen constables had formed themselves in a platoon by then at the end of the courtyard. A Head Constable and three constables were at attention on the opposite side with rifles aslope on their shoulders, ready to offer the Guard of Honour. The DSP waved his hand at the Guard and walked in. "Should you not stand and receive their salute?" "No, No. I waved at them, no? They can go and join the platoon." "Should we then inspect the men who have fallen in?" "No, let them stand. It will be good for their health."

The DSP slid his steatopygous posterior into the SI's chair and motioned at me to sit by his side. As he exchanged small talk with the Inspector over local politics, the SI gestured to some constables who started trooping in with plates and cutlery. Within a few minutes, the SI's table was covered with cashew nuts, pistachios, almonds- all in both roasted and plain versions, walnuts, raisins, biscuits- Monaco, Marie, Bourbon, pastries-chocolate and pineapple, cut fruit- apple and melon. I looked on stupefied as the DSP waded into the stuff. "Won't you have some tea? No? At least have some of these inspection nuts," he pointed at the cashews. "You don't know? It is mandatory to provide cashews to inspecting officers- hence inspection nuts," he enlightened me with a guffaw. I held back my impulse to ask him the revised nomenclature of the other nuts.

"Bring your General Diary," the DSP commanded the SI as he sprang forward to take back the teacup from him. "Good. I am happy to see that your GD is up-to-date. ASP sahib, the station GD is the master record of all that happens in a PS. That it is updated shows that this SI is doing his job promptly." *But did he not already know that you were coming for inspection and thus was not taken by surprise?* "What about the other station records?" I asked. "If the GD is up-to-date, the PS is up-to-date," he pronounced grandly. *So the eighty-odd crime records maintained in the PS are of no consequence?* The DSP saw my sceptical look and explained kindly, "when you cook rice, do you need to check all of it to ensure that it is cooked well? No! You need to test one grain only." *How would I know, I have never done any cooking!* I nodded as if wisdom was dawning over me slowly. "We will now see the parade of your men," the DSP now made ready to get up. The CI and the SI ran out and shouted at the constables to get ready for parade inspection. *How is this bunch going to march around in this confined space?*

I need not have worried as the SI, and his constables exhibited a masterclass of threading the rope through the fine needle. Left turn, right turn, left wheel, right wheel, forward, backward- every move was accomplished within that narrow strip of land between the boundary wall and the PS building. Every step fell- at the same place- regardless of the command. Forward march? No problem- left, right, left, right, left- the forward march accomplished- as the constables raised their feet and stamped them at the same place. I watched fascinated as the platoon swayed forward, backward, left and right moving only a few inches in any of the four directions.

Parade completed, we adjourned to the SI's room again. "The visit is over," the DSP intoned, "we will break for lunch." "Are you not going to write the inspection notes in the superior officers' visiting notebook?" I asked him. "There is no need. The SI will bring a neatly typed inspection note to my office later, and I will sign it there." He added graciously, "he can then paste it in the notebook." *So the SI writes his own inspection note!* The Head constable came and whispered in the CI's ear. The CI announced that the guesthouse of the local sugar mill awaited the DSP's presence.

The guesthouse was a ten-minute drive away, in the middle of a market. The General Manager of the sugar mill stood at the entrance to welcome our convoy. They had kept two rooms for the two of us. As the DSP rested in his room, I sat in my room and took out the police manual from my briefcase. I had read a few pages when I got the summons from the DSP. *The DSP is waiting for the ASP in the dining hall.* I followed the SI to the dining hall where a large table groaning under the weight of several casseroles, plates, bowls, glasses and other items of cutlery greeted me. As the CI removed cover after cover from the casseroles, I saw rice- plain boiled, fried rice-lemon and tamarind flavoured, *roties* wrapped in printed paper, curries-chicken, mutton, fish, prawns, crab, egg, vegetables- potato, peas, eggplant, the ubiquitous *sambar, rasam,* curds, pickles, fried pappadums, fruit- apples, oranges, papaya, bananas, pineapple, sweets-dry and syrupy. I felt faint. *Are you going to eat again?*

"You have to taste everything. Otherwise, the SI will take offence," the DSP warned me; "won't you?" he confirmed with the SI. "Sir, my wife has cooked everything here," the SI boasted as I quietly removed the restaurant's wrapping paper from a *roti.* I congratulated the SI on his good fortune in securing this queen of the culinary arts, the paragon of womanhood and proceeded towards the vegetarian section. The DSP was devastated to learn that I was a vegetarian and consoled me for my bad luck. As I navigated cautiously through the curries floating in oil reddened with chillies and settled for the plain curd instead, he went through each item manfully to ensure that no offence was given to the SI or his wife. "Do you have *paan*," he belched sonorously as he washed his hands. As if out of thin air, a tray of the *paan* wrapped in silver foil and packed in small, plastic sachets was produced before him. Munching happily, he announced, "you must eat *paan* for good digestion." *I am never going to eat anything when I go on tour.*

"One should take rest after a meal. A small siesta keeps you alert later in the evening. Most police work happens late in the day. Why don't you go to your room and take some rest?" the DSP advised, as he took out a *lungi* and a pair of rubber slippers from his briefcase. "But my uniform will get creased if I lie down in it," I objected. The DSP rolled his eyes and snapped his fingers at the SI, who jumped out of the DSP's room and was gone for precisely five minutes. He returned with a small packet triumphantly. I opened it to find a *lungi* and a pair of rubber slippers! I left the room as the DSP quietly farted, and the CI and the SI looked at each other to assure the DSP that they blamed each other.

I waited in my room reading the police manual till the evening. It was getting dark when the SI knocked and told me that the DSP had woken up and was ready to leave. *Before that, however, could the ASP please have some tea or coffee?* I restrained myself from yelling "NO" and went to the IISP's room who was sitting before a spread of biscuits, cookies, tea and coffee. I waited as he sipped coffee and impatiently brushed aside the CI's hand proffering a cup. The DSP sighed at this young man's impetuosity, drained his cup with a gulp and followed me as I hurried to his jeep. He waved languidly to the CI and SI as we left- and then I asked, "Sir is the inspection finally over?"

"Inspection? My dear chap, an inspection requires three days minimum. We would have stayed here for the next two days also, were I to conduct an inspection. You were obviously not ready to do that. Hence, I have confined myself to a surprise visit only."

The Reverend and I

AG Balasubramanian

I studied in a church-run college for five years, where some of my teachers were Catholic priests. They were always in cassocks and appeared to be quite distant and unapproachable. My interaction with them was minimal, limited to wishing them politely in the corridors or thanking them for some signatures in the office and so on.

I left college, moved on, and it was after nearly 15 years before another reverend came into my life. Circa late 1993. I was getting tired of living in Mumbai, and my wife was finding my frequent work-related travel tiresome. So we decided to relocate with a career shift. I spoke to one of my senior's from FPM programme in IIMA, about my need to relocate. He suggested that I should look at joining a new business school coming up in Goa. He sent in my CV and in due course, I got a handwritten letter from Fr Romualdo D'Souza SJ, then unknown to me. "Could you please come by Xavier's College, Mumbai in the evening on a particular date? I am there to interview some students for the MBA programme, and we could meet after that." said his letter.

Fr Romualdo D'Souza SJ had earlier been the Director of XLRI and the founder Director of XIM Bhubaneswar and set up the Xavier Center for Historical Research. My friend spoke of him in a hushed voice. So I was expecting a rather formal person, perhaps followed by an entourage of sorts.

What I saw, and never expected, was a tall, erect commanding person in a full-sleeved shirt and a well-polished shoe. Looking very much like a corporate executive. He was then, already very much on the wrong side of sixty, yet he looked very much younger than that. Father D'Souza was carrying a folio bag, and he came alone. He managed to get a cup of coffee each for us and then sat down to a general conversation. A lot of humming and hawing, and after a 20-30 minute conversation, we parted. I was not sure what exactly had happened. Did we just have a chat, or was it a formal interview? Nothing that I knew prepared me for an experience that a casual evening conversation could be a structured job interview. But somewhere through that conversation, he was sizing me up and decided that I would measure up in his classes.

A couple of weeks later, a letter came home by post. Handwritten at some airport. Appointing me as an associate professor in the business school at Goa. I was supposed to join in July, just in time to start the new academic year. I became the first professor to be formally appointed at the Goa Institute of Management. The other six already teaching there were the founding team who moved with him from XIM to GIM.

I moved from Mumbai to Goa towards the end of June 1994. It was my first time in Goa. It cost me almost everything I had in the bank to pack and ship my belongings to Goa. After paying off the truck driver, I hardly had any money to my credit. The truck owner was a known guy – but his driver insisted on getting cash to buy diesel to drive back to Mumbai. The organization I had been working for was yet to settle my final dues. So here I was in Panjim, in the first-floor apartment of a building on the banks of Mandovi River. All my furniture was still in gunnysack parcels strewn around, and the wife was running a fever. We went into Panjim to the first hospital we could find and met a doctor. By now, whatever little money I had in my purse was also gone! We decided to stay in the guest room we had and go back to the apartment the next day. I was getting seriously worried about our financial situation. I was loudly wondering to my wife about how we were going to tide over the first month in a strange town!

The next morning my wife suggested that we try and put the new apartment into some shape and order. I took off my shirt and got to work unpacking the first of the packages. There was a knock on the door and in walked an unexpected guest. It was Fr D'Souza who had come by to find out how his new professor was settling in! That was the second time I was meeting him. I didn't know where to ask him to sit. My cane sofas were still in their sacking, and there were boxes full of books and stuff stacked everywhere. I couldn't even borrow a chair, as I was the first person to move into the building. All the other professors were yet to move in.

He just decided to settle down on top of the gunnysack covered chair! I hastily introduced my wife to him. She quickly apologized on our behalf for his discomfort, but he just waved them away. He then asked me how much it cost me to move my things to Goa. He pulled out a chequebook from his bag and wrote out a cheque for me. Wow – Godsend money!

Fr D'Souza then got talking to my wife, asking her how she would cook? There was no gas connection, but I had the papers from my Mumbai connection. He immediately drove me in his car to the gas agency and stood in front of the gas agency guy. That man was embarrassed that Fr D'Souza decided to go to him personally and suggested that he could have just called him. Fr D'Souza just grinned at him and suggested if the agency would hurry up with the connection, he could get rid of him!! It took 10 minutes to get the gas connection, and my kitchen was up and running the next day.

Here was a man who had rebuilt one premier educational institution, set up two from scratch and on the way to building his next one – the Goa Institute of Management. All of this in a single lifetime. Most people would have just sat down and put their feet up after one. He went on to be honoured with the Padma Shri.

Fr D'Souza used to drive himself everywhere he needed to go and to get us whatever we needed. He personally came home to check on and welcome me. He sat on a dusty sack covered chair. He wrote me a cheque for expenses saving me the embarrassment of asking him or borrowing money, knowing a young man like me would have little savings. I have known some people with far less achievement who stand on a lot more formalities.

In the initial years of GIM, there was a severe cash-flow problem and shortage of money. Revenue came in once in three months as students paid fees once every term. Still, salaries and other expenses had to be met every month! He would always make sure our salaries were paid but not always on the first of the month. However, a single income person like me and a couple of others would get paid on time. He would delay the payment for some of the professors who were couples both working in GIM. Of those, he would pay the two female professors on time but delay paying the husband's salaries. Perhaps this was his own idea of gender sensitivity; much before the word had become fashionable?

In that first year, I had finished my quota of teaching in the first two terms. I was hoping to take the third term a bit easy. Fr D'Souza walked into my office and wanted to know if I would teach a particular elective on Performance Management that students were asking for. I had been in a semi academic-industry job previously and did not have any material ready.

So I told him it would take me a couple of months to assemble the teaching material. This was a time when there was just a couple of halfway decent booksellers in Goa and access to management books was limited. The internet was still a few years away. We just had about a fortnight or so to get ready for the course, and it looked reasonably uphill to me. Fr D'Souza asked me what books I would need to start out. I told him TV Rao's book would help. We had just one copy in the library. He mumbled something and left, and I thought I was off the hook.

Four or five days later, the GIM librarian let me know that about half a dozen copies of TV Rao's book were waiting for me! A day or two later, a bundle of cases arrived from XLRI from a professor who taught that course there. So come the third term, I was teaching a class of students the Performance Management elective! I recall that the textbooks were shared two to a book by the students. Just to rewind a bit. We did not have a telephone connection in GIM in those days as we had just moved to the campus given to us by the Goa Government. So the very afternoon Fr D'Souza spoke to me, he drove to Panjim and made two telephone calls. One was to Prof. Rao to ask him to courier the copies of his book to us pronto. The other call was to pull in a favour from a professor at XLRI. So, how did Fr D'Souza know I would agree to teach the course? He never compelled me to do it as he knew I had already done my share of teaching. What he did was to make sure I had no more excuses left not to teach it!

Here was a man who had no ego issues and never stood on formality. He was always focused on delivering value to the students. Everything else was incidental. He kept his achievements in the past and always focused on the present.

All this was learning-in-action for me, a professor who teaches organizational behaviour and people management. It was a revelation for someone who teaches stuff like institution building, empathy, people focus, gender sensitivity, and creating enabling work environment!!

All these incidents came back to me recently when I heard that Fr Romualdo D'Souza had passed away on 1st November 2019. He said goodbye to this world at the ripe age of 95 years, having done more than a fair share for one man's lifetime. Rest in peace, Reverend!

Career Limiting Move

Sanjeev Kotnala

Cricket is a religion in India. And most of us at some time in our life have tried our hand at the game. Here is an episode out of HTA the leading agency in Delhi in the early 90s, Hindustan Thompson Associates, now called JWT. HTA was as much into cricket as it was into planning, and that says a lot. There are stories of Denis Joseph bowling a beamer to a client or Shankar Rajan playing a sedate inning. One person who kept the tradition alive at Delhi office was Sanjay Bali. He was the captain who religiously followed cricket, ensured HTA took part in the Media Transasia tournament and won it a few times.

But when Sunil Gupta took over Delhi office, cricket took to a new dimension. Sunil Gupta other than being a great advertising person, was also a theatre actor and now has acted in some movies too. Oh, by the way, he was one of the finalists when ESPN ran the search for the next TV commentator. He lost to Prakash Narsimhan due to age factor,

In Sunil Gupt's regime, there was never any shortage of Cricket gear or money to book the groud. This was when Delhi office team toured Kolkatta, and HTA won the 'Media Transasia Agency cricket' trophy. I was part of the team- and do not have any significant contribution to talk of.

What I am sharing seems like a small insignificant episode that is well known within the HTA Jhandewalan fraternity of that time, the early 90s. Sanjay Bali reminded me of it in one of his comments on my face-book account.

I met Sunil Gupta in Delhi at one of the E4M CMO League last year, even he referred to it but knowingly said he did not much remember what it was all about.

So here, it's for you Sunil.

It was just another Saturday. HTA Delhi and IMRB were playing a friendly game at the well-maintained cricket ground at the SriFort sports complex. It was a friendly game. Even some of the team members were swapped to make a match of it. In friendly matches, It was not rare for the teams to realise that they were short of players and they must borrow from the other side.

I am not sure of what all happened and who won or lost that day. The incident that is imprinted in my mind happened towards the fag end of the game.

I was the Main Umpire, and Sanjay Bali was at that time was the other umpire Some bowler (name not important) was trying to get the HTA team wickets. He was bowling flat off-spin. Ravi Verma, the art director, was at the runner's end and Sunil Gupta was facing the ball.

For the last 3 balls, Sunil Gupta had moved across the wicket and comfortably padded the balls outside the off stump. As expected, there was a loud appeal from the team every time the pad met the ball.

When it happened, Sunil Gupta would shake his head and show his back to the umpire, that was me. All the 3 times I gave him not-out as no way the ball would have hit the stumps.

Ball number 4. The bowler came in a bit faster than regular, and this time looped the ball. The ball bowled from the edge of the crease. It took its time, Sunil Gupta moved outside the line, it pitched on and around the off-stump and instead of holding its line or moving toward the leg just straightened.

Sunil had stepped forward and moved outside the line. He held his bat held behind his right pad and offered no stroke. The ball hit him below the knee roll. The appeal was loud. Louder than any other time. In my opinion, the ball would have crashed between the off and the middle stump. Sunil in a practised routine moved out and showed me his back. He was confident he was not out. And to his surprise, I raised my finger.

No one gives Sunil out on the cricket field. Not like this. Not until unless he is bowled (you still had a chance to call it a NO ball) or is clearly caught. LBW was definitely not something you considered while Sunil Gupta batted. It was defined as a CLM (Career Limiting move). But then he was a batsman, and in my opinion, he was out. So, I did what came naturally to me, raised my finger.

Sunil glared at me, and I held to my decision.

He was now visibly getting agitated. And when he gets angry, he turns red, the veins in his throat bulge.

He threw his bat and shouted at me. 'Do you know how to play? Mr Kotnala this was not out'.

I held my ground. And said something that people later said was suicidal. 'OUT, this behaviour does not seem right for the head of the largest agency in town. As for cricket, I have played at a higher level than you could have- and mind you on the field I am the umpire and you just a player- get out of the field'.

Sensing the situation getting out of control and Sanjay Bali stepped in between us. He was holding me back. Sunil after showing his displeasure picked the bat he had thrown and walked out.

I looked at Ravi, and he in the lowest possible voice concurred with my decision. He also felt that from the runner's point of view- which is the second-best position in such instances, Sunil was out. However, he was smart and would not accept it in public.

I was shunted to the leg umpire position. That's where I remained for the rest of the match.

As was usual in advertising circles, post-match there was beer and some snacks. I coolly gulped down mine; I knew I was right, and Ravi had confirmed it.

However, my satisfaction was short-lived. Ravi Verma tells me, he was out boss, And I should not have given him out. You know how passionate he is about his game.

Anyway, I was advised by many HTA people not to come to the office for the next few days till Sunil cooled down, or if I was in office, remain out of sight. However, it would be best if I kept a signed A4 sheet with my resignation ready.

Well, I did come to the office, and nothing happened. However, though Sunil may say he did not remember, for the next two to three months, I could sense an apparent coldness from Sunil's side, With time even that died.

I am not sure, should I have not given Sunil out, it was in any way a friendly match between two teams of the same organisation. Or did I do the right thing? There was no option of DRS. The mobile was still to be launched.

However, as far as I was concerned, I did the right thing. Differentiated between the organisation and the game. I kept life very modular. At least I felt good.

Language Breaks Barriers

N. Subramaniam

As a Private Equity investment professional, my job was to find the "hidden gems" worth investing, to multiply investor money.

Using all the knowledge gained, along with around 10 years of experience under my belt, I was following up on what looked like an excellent opportunity.

Here's a little background: The promoters were Malayali's from Kerala, and settled in Mumbai for over 30 years. The Finance Director was a Gold medalist CA who hailed from Bangalore, Karnataka and was considered a prodigy in Income Tax.

The company was in the Fast Moving Consumer Goods Sector, with great financial ratios: about Rs 800 Million in revenues and a solid Rs 200 million in net profits after tax- 25% Net!!! Growth in the past three years was upward of 18% pa. This was a transaction to chase and close as mandated by my investment committee.

I was apprehensive based on my training because of a curious red flag. The company paid no income taxes while not belonging to any sector that enjoyed concessions. At that time, concessional IT rates were given only to Export-oriented Units and Information Technology service companies, which also was export albeit of services. Many IT companies misused them (no tangible goods you see) to launder 'black' money into kosher profits of an enterprise at no cost.

My partner, also an IIMA graduate analyzed the company with his limited financial knowledge and brief experience at Hindustan Lever Ltd (HLL, now HUL) as a summer trainee. He created a checklist of questions that would help us understand this situation.

During our first interaction with the company, my partner asked many questions notable among which was "What is your credit rating process vis a vis Distributors?" He had noticed a disproportionately small amount of receivables and correlating this with the systems he had studied in the HLL credit control department, came up with this intelligent killer question. The stunningly simple answer came from the promoter-"What credit Limit? We don't extend credit!" The receivables were Demand Drafts in transit from distributors. Advance fax copies of such drafts were already in possession of the company. During the end of the year, they would ship only against such confirmations of Demand Drafts in transit. Hence whatever receivables at the year-end were cleared max, by 7th April of the Following financial year.

They explained zero income taxes by the manufacturing unit being in a classified backward area with concessions (Pondicherry). According to the potential investing company, such questions of huge importance but which had simple explanations frustrated the promoter. He voiced his concern about the proposed partnership with our fund. His main worry was the challenges of partnering with such a 'green' team. A team with no idea about subtle nuances of practical business dynamics never mind what institution they are from, or the qualifications they hold.

Facing outright rejection, I called and requested another meeting with the promoter, which he reluctantly accepted. The Director Finance empathizing with a fellow CA (me!)

had managed to persuade him. When I reached their offices, I realized I was slotted into the last appointment for the day. I stood between him and a relaxed evening at home after a hard day's work. His car had collected his daughter from school, and they were just waiting to go. Father and daughter (possibly studying commerce electives in Standard XII) were deep in conversation. I started by praising the business they had created. I talked of the brand Shine, the magic of four, which they had established. Its catchy jingle, amazing tax structuring enabling reinvestment for growth, the Mumbai weather, and traffic ...anything that came to mind.

Meanwhile, the daughter asked her father a question on something that I had said, in Malayalam. Even as he started on his explanation, I broke in into Malayalam and clarified my point. After that, the conversation switched to Malayalam, and I asked for another chance to understand the business. I appealed to his experience and at the same time, defended my team. I politely asked him: "how can you expect us to understand and fathom a business in 15 minutes which has taken you and your team 15 years to build?". He nodded in agreement.

Moreover, having heard the management-speak proudly about its Sales force as a strength, I asked to go with a Salesman for a day and walk the market to understand the depths of the business contours. We closed the meeting with the understanding that the investment team and I had been granted a second chance to study and understand the business.

I was to go to Bangalore and spend a day on the Devanahalli beat. When I reached Bangalore, Director Finance was there to receive me. He was curious to know how I had managed to convince the promoter for a second chance. I gracefully attributed it to his efforts at having got me a second chance to prove myself. He was persistent and keen to know what exactly

I discussed, and I summarized it for him. As we drove up to the distributor office to join the salesman in his van, he got a call from his wife. Cellular telephony had just been introduced then. He spoke loudly to her in a dialect of Kannada called Tulu. Once the phone conversation was over, I casually resumed the conversation in Kannada and that really resonated with him. He was a small-town boy who had fought his way to excellence. He had always been intimidated by English-speaking business associates. This attempt of mine to put him at ease, and speak to him in 'his language' was a welcome change for him. He found it hard and amusing to accept that an IIM graduate was actually speaking in Kannada in a business meeting when it was not his mother tongue!

I got into the van with the salesman, and we started on the Devanahalli beat. As soon as I did so, the Director Finance called the promoter confirming I had just done what I threatened to do! Go with the salesman on a beat for a day!

It seems this going on the beat with the salesman was the clincher. The promoter decided I would make a good partner (as part of a firm) since I spoke the language and I was keen to learn. For him, sitting in a van and walking the streets in the heat!! Was physical hardship?

My most significant learning that day was really humbling. My CA, ICWA, ACS, IIM qualifications stood me in good stead for desk-based analysis of Businesses and Balance Sheets. However, my real qualification was my ability to speak in Tamil, Telugu, Malayalam, Kannada, Hindi and English. It helped me connect with business counterparts in a non-intimidating way! It was a Eureka moment, and I set out to pursue vigorously even more language skills and have since acquired a working knowledge of Bengali and Gujarati.

Special Need

Srikumar

It was one of those days, when I had this interesting walk-in customer. At that time, I was Customer Service and Service Quality, Country head (India) in a well-known Multinational bank. My role involved engaging with customers across all the consumer banking products, including bank accounts, loans, credit cards, to list a few.

As the country head, in my role, it was routine to get dragged into severe customer service issues. They would crop up every week with weird unpredictability. I would be expected to analyse them with my seniors, go to the root cause and then decide on the stance to take. These issues rarely involved "Walk-in" customers.

One of the days, I was interrupted by a call from the security team telling me of a walk-in customer who demanded to see me. I had just finished a meeting and had time on hand. So, instead of directing him to someone else, I asked the security to escort him to my cabin.

I could see him walking with the security towards my cabin. He was a well-dressed gentleman of around thirty-five years and confident of his surroundings.

When he entered my room, I gestured him to take the seat. Then as a routine, I tried starting a conversation about the problem he was facing.

It was then that I realised the gentleman was deaf and dumb. He was showing me his credit card. He had some issue with it, and I could not understand it. I was at a total loss. Forget taking a decision and helping him, I did not have any clue as to what the issue or the problem was.

To buy some time, I offered him coffee and water and gestured him to wait for me. I was in quite a daze. It was a human reality. It had never struck me before that we also have customers with special needs.

I needed a minute to compose my thoughts. My first reaction was to take the customer contact information and then have a sign-language expert meet him later. I was not sure whose special need was greater, the customer in my cabin or me who had never considered this possibility.

I stepped out to think and find some solution. Involuntarily with a slightly parched throat, I moved to the water cooler. I was simply confused, as I had no answer. I did not know what to do. There at the cooler, I met this excellent co-worker, Rama. I had pooled her in on a special project for some time.

She saw the perplexed expression in my face, a sense of helplessness. Rama going out of her work scope and hierarchy asked me what was bothering me? I felt that there was no point in telling her anything. How could she be of any help? However, as I was cornered for some advice, I shared my predicament. And I told Rama what I planned to do. She volunteered to solve the issue and requested that she should be allowed to speak with the customer.

So Rama and I went back in. One can call the subsequent events as fate, luck, or divine intervention.

To my utter amazement, Rama conversed with that person in sign language, and in a few minutes solved his complaint. It was so simple. The gentleman had misunderstood some feature of our credit card. He was quite clear that the mistake was of the bank. Rama took her time and convinced him that was not the case.

A few days later, my manager (country head), a very tough person but with an inherently soft heart, came to me. For a change, he was smiling. He showed me news clipping, where the very same customer had spoken in glowing terms about his entire banking experience. The customer was amazed that a large multinational bank with huge customer base was concerned about special need customers. And that they even had sign language experts to converse. How was he to know the situation? He had watched me walking to the cooler and speaking with Rama. In his mind, I had walked to my sign-language expert to solve his problem.

There was an eye-opener for me. I sensed we don't really know our work team. People have the most amazing skills and capabilities. Rama, in fact, was the topper in ASL and SEE. ASL is the American Sign Language, a complex visual-spatial language that is used by the Deaf community in the United States & English-speaking parts of Canada. It is a linguistically complete, natural language. SEE stands for Signed Exact English; it is a system of manual sign and gesture communication that strives to be an exact representation of English vocabulary and grammar.

After this, when I started looking, I found we had in our office a qualified fire equipment person, a home nurse, a musical instruments repair expert, and so on. All in the team that has been with me for a long time. Their talent and expertise were hidden because we never tried to find out and explore. At least for me, Rama interaction with the customer was a real aha moment for me. After that, in my entire career, I have tried finding these hidden talents and expertise. Trust me, it helped me a lot.

On a serious note, when I look back at this instance, I realise we have customers with special needs for all our products and services. It is same with fellow employees, our vendors, our family, the local chai-walla, and everyone else in any business. How we overlook them while designing the service and products or even customer care interaction. It is our duty as a brand or service provider to be inclusive and knows how to react- interact and handle them. Sometimes all it takes is a patient hearing and logical explanation to solve the problem.

However much you plan, there is an indefinable something called "fate", or "luck", or "divine intervention" which pops up to help, at the most unexpected times.

....

Aside: When I checked later with the security person how he knew the customer wanted to meet me, he had a simple explanation. Sir, I did not understand him and thought I should take him to someone senior.

The Shoot at Madh Island

Sanjeev Kotnala

'What kind of photographer are you, everyone can shoot when the light is good, a good one should be able to shoot in a bad light' I shouted at the photographer.

....

I was less than a week into real advertising. Fresh after completing the 3-month rigorous management training programme MMTP-II. Dr Naganand Kumar and CM Ramesh (UNCLE TOM), had ensured that all the graduates of MMTP-II were charged enough to make a mark in Indian advertising. We believed everything was possible. We were going to be the brand and advertising saviour of the country.

In my very first week of formally reporting to the Ahmedabad branch, I was sent to Mumbai on a shoot for the Brand; Mayur Suitings. It was my first official trip and my first shoot. With no-one to brief me and with a clear objective to get the result, I was finally going to Mumbai, the centre of Indian advertising. Oh, I have finally arrived in the glamorous world of Advertising.

Mumbai shoot coordinator had taken care of most of the things. I was like a proper client servicing executive was there to ensure nothing went wrong. And in case anyone from the client-side reported for the shoot, to keep them entertained. Get the shoot done and get back to Ahmedabad with the results.

The city was new, and I had never had any run-in with the Mumbai fickle weather. The shoot was lined up at Madh Island with the ace photographer Denzil Sequaria.

We had booked one of those Bungalows on the beach and were shooting next to the pool within the property. It was daytime, and the light was deteriorating. Denzil was asking everyone to hurry-up.

Finally, when the models were ready, the weather decided to play spoilsport.

Denzil waited for the light to improve. And when nothing happened to his liking and with the sun also slowly making its way to the horizon, he decided to call off the shoot at 1600 Hrs.

Now, please understand. As per this newly baked Account Executive, there was no problem, people were taking short cuts and not willing to apply their mind.

There was enough light. Why was Denzil making all this fuss. Anyway, him calling off the shoot was against my objective. It seemed the perfect place to tell him who the boss was. My IIMA taught mind was further sharpened and turned into assertive one at the MMTP-II. I was ready with management skills and understanding.

I have already confessed I was new to the system. I was unaware of the protocol at the location, including who takes the decisions. The only thing I knew was Client Servicing has to deliver on the requirements of the Brand.

So, when Denzil said it was bad light, it was not ok with me. I also realised that as a team leader, you do not create a scene before the team. If you have to take someone to task, it must be done as much in privacy as possible. So, I spoke to Denzil and took him to a corner, where I believed we were not visible to others.

An exciting conversation took place.

Me: Denzil is the light really bad.

Denzil: Yeah baba I know, what do you think.

Me: But, we must shoot. Everything is ready.

Denzil: I can't shoot. We will not get the right results.

Me: But if we don't shoot, we will get no results.

Denzil: We will shoot tomorrow.

Me: If you don't mind, give me your camera, and I will shoot.

Denzil: You know how to shoot… and what will you do.

ME: No… you tell me, and I will shoot. Anyway, we have lost the model sitting fee, travel, stay, location and your fee. If we now shoot in this bad light, we will lose just the cost of the 3-4 film rolls. (it is much before digital became the format of default). If I get at least one workable transparency (TP) – it would have been worth it.

I remember the stare Denzil gave me. And for some silly reason, he smiled while handing me his camera. The camera was loaded with a large telephoto lens and had numerous notations and dials. He explained to me a bit of it, maybe the minimalistic things that I better know to take care of the camera. I heard him out with deep concentration. I was focussed. And then bravely I started shooting with the models. It was experimentation at its peak.

We must have shot some 24-30 frame with the models at the same location. This was after all a trial.

Then we saw the results after a week. Philip, the art director at Mudra Ahmedabad, agreed that there was reason enough for me to have made a fool out of myself. Yet, there were by a miracle, two frames that could be used. They were not the best but good enough for the poster. And with one of those two transparencies, we went on to create a 20X30 inch poster for trade promotion.

Denzil and I shot many more campaigns and posters for Mayur and Vimal suitings. But, this little incident at Mud Island created a different kind of understanding between us. There were many more incidents of varying nature, leading to some humour and some learning. I learnt that one can always do an open-eyed conscious trade-off, sometimes they work and sometimes they don't, and you will only know if you are willing to experiment.

SECTION-D
Life

The Coffee
that Changed My Life

Sanjeev Kotnala

It was early winter. I remember it still after so many years, to be precise 40 years. I know because the image of her looking at me with that surprised and irritated expression is intact in my mind. And she was wearing the navy-blue school sweater. Her sweater even had a wavy looking white line at the border, hugging her healthy frame.

She was Bina, my classmate at Kendriya Vidhyalaya GCF Estate, Jabalpur. She was down to earth and equally favourite among girls and boys. She was decent in studies and was what one can also term as a sportsperson.

There was Subir Biswas, Ajay Mehra and I kind of a team. Each one aware of the feelings; the soon to be an adult type of feelings. Love-shove type of feelings. Interested and okay kind of feeling.

Those days there was no mobile. No WhatsApp where the status could be updated or video request could be made. Even at home, most of us did not have phone connections and to make any call had to go to some Kirana shop. The school was co-education, that meant that boys and girls sat in the same classroom and attended the same sports and assembly. Other than that, it was neither the era of sitting with hands held tight or trading of bold kisses. Or maybe it was not my area of expertise.

Bina Bhat, I liked her. I wanted to befriend her. Oh, make that more than just a friend. As we were friends, we studied in the same class, sometimes we even cycled together after school till the place we were forced to different ways, I sometimes called her home to ask for some books and notes. It was always me asking for them. And then, we both have cycled together to Ajay Mehra's house.

Then came the time for selection of school teams for various sports who would go for the zonal round. Bina was already in the Volleyball and Kho-Kho team. I had thought of going for the kho-kho selection, and then I saw the way Sunil Nair, Virendra Chandola and Anil dodged and played the game. I realised it was not for me.

There was still Badminton. A game I knew I was decent with. Bina was expected to even go for zonal selection in Badminton along with Poonam Sharma. Ajay Mehra was also participating. The trial was held at YMCA courts in Sadr Bazar. I was present there with a newly bought set of racquets.

The guys and girls started warming up. And I could hear the sound of the game. They were smashing the poor shuttle and my confidence at the same time. I knew that if I even tried to be on the court, I will make a fool of myself, and that was surely not advisable before Bina. So, I just tagged along. Poonam and Ajay made to the team.

I just kept waiting and watching from the sidelines.

I was trying to gain the confidence to talk to Bina and ask her out of coffee. Soon, the zonal were over, and the team was back at the school. There were various stores of people finding their girl-boy friend during the sports competition.

Then one day, I finally got enough courage to catch her alone next to the Physical Education storeroom. I think she had come to collect the volleyball and me to meet her. As she locked the room and stepped outside, I stopped her.

'Bina, will you come for coffee with me.'

'What' she asked as if she did not hear it the first time.

'Will you come for coffee with me.'

'Why'

'Just like that.'

'No, tell me why I should come and have coffee with you.'

'Because we are friends'

'So, why ask.'

I had no answer, but she was not finished.

'Listen, I have been noticing you. You are a decent guy. However, you are not good looking. You are average in studies, play no sports, what makes you even think that I will come for coffee with you?' And she starts walking with the volleyball spinning her fingers.

I am finished, but it is not over yet. I turn back and almost yell at Bina, which stops her on her tracks.

'Is that the problem. Okay, I promise you I will always get better marks than the last exam in my life, all my life.'

She looked at me, smiled at my statement and left.

I believe she was the reason. Something snapped within me. I started focusing on studies. So in my twelfth grade, I got more marks than I got in tenth grade. In BSc, I got more than what I earned in twelfth grade. In BSc more than what I got in XIIth, then the gold medal at engineering and finally IIM Ahmedabad.

Now, when I pause to reflect. I see such incidents differently. I realize, after my Mother, it is Bina who is responsible for what I achieved in life.

Just think. What if, she had accepted the coffee invitation? What if I had not made that overconfident rejoinder to her? What, if I had not taken the statement seriously enough? What if I had stopped keeping my promise to someone I barely knew and only met once again in entire life.

I know, my life would have been different.

A Life Kissed Me 'Goodbye'

SP Singh

They say death is inevitable. From the moment you are born, the only thing sure is your death. One day death will come. Everything else in life is just a possibility and probability. Yet we fear the sure shot thing and chase probabilities. Yes, it happened to me too. A life kissed me goodbye forever and made me realise how lucky I am to be alive today.

Being alive and conscious is the greatest thing. I believe we are not in this world accidentally. A person can be alive at many levels. At a physiological level is one of the most apparent levels of living. Pulse, heartbeat and movement of body parts are some of the common indicators of life. However, I have come to realise that there can be more parameters. I not only feel my heartbeat but hear it as well. My heart pumping blood to my brain is new music to my ears. It continually reminds me of me being conscious and alert.

I believe, if I am breathing, I am of some value to someone in this world, and hence my net – Networth is positive.

Life will one day come to a standstill. We accept and acknowledge – someday all of us have to meet the Almighty. This meeting will happen only once. Still, we hold our head high in the belief of longevity. Days go on seamlessly.

I celebrate with my near and dear ones; the ups and downs of life, mountains of happiness, and valleys of despair. I choose to stand-alone and try to climb new heights. In this journey, I had a brief encounter with Almighty, and it was disconcerting.

It taught me more than any other life experience. I realised we are socially conditioned to a level that lines between action and inaction get blurred. In fact, our response rate is conditioned.

So, let me get to that incident, episode of my life imprinted in my memory.

We live in Gurgaon's most modern part and share the boundary wall with our immediate neighbours, they had also moved in almost twenty-five years back. There is a concrete wall between our two houses separating us however there has never been a wall between two homes. As life moved on, their home became an empty nest. The son and the daughter moved abroad, and now the old couple live by themselves with minimal interference with anyone's life. You could say for both of them that there are two bodies and one soul living next to our house.

Maybe it is in the name of the society we live in. Sushant Lok, it is very quiet in the afternoon after everyone has left for work. Shanti prevails in the surroundings with occasional sounds of the street dog's occasional reminder of his presence. You can barely spot any soul moving around the building. If anyone is missing a day's work they will mostly be indoors.

This happened one fine morning, one could hear the wind blowing, in an otherwise silent society. I was working on the terrace of my two storey house. It was always my passive dream to beautify the terrace garden, and finally, I was giving it shape. It was around 10.15 am when I was called for help. Our neighbour's wife was shouting for help. There was desperation in those loud shouts. I could feel anxiety dominating even though it was faint to me. Someone again shouted, and this time the attempt was deliberate and emphatic. It made me go to the terrace wall and look down. I saw my neighbour's wife whom we fondly call "Aunty" was at the door asking for immediate attention as Uncle was not feeling well. Sensing anxiety and desperation in her voice, made me leave my handheld drill machine and race down the stairs to help. In a moment, I reached their house. I was pointed to go to the bedroom where I saw our most favourite Uncle was lying motionless. I first thought he is just taking rest as he was not keeping well for past few days. I tried to feel his pulse. There was none.

I tried to feel the heartbeat. No luck. I started to press uncle's chest. Nothing happened. I got worried, and so did Aunty sensing panic in my face.

As a last resort, I tried mouth-to-mouth respiration and every possible first aid act that I knew of. I was into action then and knew there was no time at hand and being alone was no advantage.

Feeling helpless, I rushed to the nearby clinic where we often go for general medical help in case of small ailments. In the middle of the market where neither the sunbeams reach nor does the network connects, the commercial activity starts only after 11 am. I ran to the market which we frequent regularly, hardly a 10 minutes walk. Taking out the car from parking would not have helped as would have taken more time. I almost lost my breath even after running a 100 meters sprint only to find that The Doctor had not reported to his clinic yet. His assistant was busy doing routine medical tests and collecting samples. Since I was breathless, I held him and narrated the situation in my broken voice. I was desperately begging for help. Some help.

I was shocked. I could not believe what the assistant said. Did he really say NO, that he can't help, 'Doctor Sahib Abhi Nahi Aye'.

Feeling the assistant was anyway not willing to take any risk and help, I rushed back to my uncle just to try the second time. This time too, the signals I was looking for, as a testimony of him being alive were completely missing.

I felt the light went off !.

I again rushed to Doctor's clinic, this time, luckily the Doctor was there.

Here I was breathless and narrating the situation, crying for emergency help. But it did not make the Doctor move any faster. He calmly gave instructions on the phone. Asked his assistant to get the ECG instrument. And then he asked me to lead him to our neighbour's house. We both walked and as I wanted to run back, felt Doctor was walking even slower than Snail. (or it was me being impatient and wanting him to run too !)

Finally, we both reached and I was calmer this time, as there was professional right there. By this time more people had reached the house too. We all felt by this time, there was nothing he could do. He declared our uncle dead. What they say "Found dead on arrival".

Shock and despair spread in the room.

Everybody was shocked.

There is no record of the event. There won't be. No one will question how and why it took so long for help to arrive. No one is there asking, calibrating or monitoring the response rate. It is not part of someone's KRA. What is the ideal rate of response? There are no matrices to measure it. And that is when and where a split second can make the difference between life and death.

Now, and often, I try to roll back and add 'challenges of "real life" to my life. I realise our responsiveness is conditional.

Why should my responsiveness to any event be conditioned by society? Why should it be non-judgmental? We all must be the first line of doctors. We must know the necessary first aid and emergency assistance. We must be expert in MTMR; Minimal Time Maximum Results. Not only we should know it, but we must also be able to deliver when called to action.

The quality of the response and rate of reaction can make a massive difference to the outcome.

It does matter. How quickly and strongly do you take charge of the situation?

Practise Becoming

Giri Giridhar

These two words have defined the way I live. They simply mean that Success as an endpoint is usually elusive – so *Practise Becoming* is a way which makes the journey meaningful and focusses on improvement all the time.

My earliest recollection of life was sleeping next to my grandfather while he narrated to me Shakespeare, Dickens etc. Early schooling at Airport High School at Sahar Mumbai. Walking to school with Umesh and catching fish in gutters during the rains. Later studied in DAV school in Chennai while dad lived in Mumbai. Studies, quizzing was everything. Stayed at the Taj Colaba in 1978, courtesy Bournvita Quiz Contest. How was I to know, one day, I will be CFO at Taj.

Life of Contradictions

I was born in Chennai, but I am not a Tamilian. Marathi is my mother tongue – from the Dakshini Marathi clan. We descended from a breakaway group of Marathas who migrated to south India post the Chatrapati Shivaji era a few hundred years ago. The clan is small, but the diaspora is spread throughout the world.

I pursued a tortuous CA course by day with college in the evening. Thought I will become an auditor; went to IIM Ahmedabad instead. On passing out, I thought I will be a banker and joined ICICI, which precisely lasted 5 days.

Born in a very conservative Brahmin family - I don't smoke, drink little and take no drugs. Who would have thought I would go on to build a career in vices. Selling cigarettes at ITC, booze at Diageo (Johnnie Walker, Smirnoff *et al*), drugs at Merck & Co, the US Pharma Giant. And now, I run a hotel business at Taj.

Came from a conservative family where my mother was a matchmaker for my community. But I met Laxmi, a Tamil girl from Hyderabad, Andhra Pradesh. Fortunately, love prevailed.

Our daughter Raksheta is a banker, an economics masters from LSE. And a painter. And our son Hrishikesh is a guitarist primarily. With an economist masters-to-be from LSE.

I am a dreamer and a realist. Can be an optimist and paranoid. Soft-spoken but can also blow up.

A lifetime of Learnings

In 1998, our son Hrishikesh was born. Cesarean section. Two days later, Laxmi developed a complication, and she underwent abdominal surgery again. Laxmi was in the ICU and our infant son in the pediatric ward. The nurse would take him to Laxmi every two hours for a feed. A mother's love to breastfeed the newborn in the ICU. It is probably the most significant event in my life.

My first significant life learning was at Guntur, where the leaf tobacco division of ITC was seen as the mother company, making a difference to thousands of tobacco farmers. Two years ago, I saw the same impact that Tata Steel has at Jamshedpur.

In Dubai, at ITC, I learnt that unbridled business growth without safeguards is unsustainable. Growth and sustainability go hand in hand.

As an investment banker, I learnt the importance of personal credibility and track record where nothing but delivery will ensure you will ever get a paid mandate from a client.

Diageo taught me how to run a global business, taught me - Be Proud of what you do, meaning don't do anything which will not make you proud.

At Wockhardt, I helped to drive profitability and grow market cap 18x in 30 months. It made me understand that transformations are possible. It gave me hope.

Merck taught me that empathy is everything. George W Merck said medicine is for patients; not for profits, as long as you remember that profits automatically follows.

At Tatas, I learn every day what outstanding customer service is; what adhering to the highest forms of ethics and integrity are.

Meandering

Singapore 2002, where I was working for Diageo. It was the first time I was working with Brits, Indonesians, Chinese, Filipinos. Unceasing travel.

London 2005, when I was working as a Business Development Director. Travel continued - Caracas one week, Tokyo another. And everywhere in between.

Discovered a love for tasting Indian cuisine in different cities around the world. A *'dal tadka'* in Moscow was different from the one in Inverness. I discovered that male stewards in these restaurants were from India or Bangladesh, the females were local. Russian girls in lehengas dancing to Bollywood music. An economics student by day, pole dancing by night at Rasputin at Moscow. A drink at Cloud Nine on the 86th floor of Grand Hyatt at Shanghai. Bar hopping around the world. *Thirtham.*

And Thirtha Prasadam - Weekly Satsang on Saturdays in London were the norm. Chanting *'Hanuman Chalisa'* at Snake's home. Saibaba now my spiritual Guru.

Humility & Caring

Dad died in 2011. I regret, I never did spend enough time with him. He spent a lifetime working for the government. With a transferable job, he spent many years away from the family – we grew up with mom and grandparents.

My father in law has a significant influence on me. At 92, he still walks with a straight gait, does crosswords, and keenly watches sports. He is not much educated, but his grandchildren study at Carnegie Mellon to doctorates in Europe to LSE.

Laxmi has been the diligent homemaker, carer for kids, they are what they are with her care.

Our parents and Laxmi have taught me humility and caring.

Peripatetic

A life long traveller - tethered by love and authenticity.

I keep walking.

Milo Kotnala

Sanjeev Kotnala

11th December is MILO KOTNALA's birthday. That's not the actual date. However, the date Milo Kotnala came home in 2017.

Milo Kotnala is family. The latest member of KOTNALA's of Kandivali. And he is part of this book, because of the experiences I have. And let me start from the beginning.

My daughter Preetica had been after us to get a pet at home. I was dead against it. Childhood memories don't die that easily. A phobia is implanted just because some dog chased me way early in my life, the incident led to cynophobia ; fear of the dogs.

My wife Neha was worried about the possible nuisance the dog could create. The care a pet would need. And she knew it will finally come on her to take responsibility. Somehow she came around to accepting the demand. And I stayed with the clear dictate, 'In my house only one dog could live'.

Preetica held to her ground. All she wanted on her birthday was a pet at home. Trust me, I tried my best. But, then in a moment of weakness sometime in November 2017, the father's love for his daughter gave in to her demand. I had held my ground for too long and then promised my daughter that we would get a pet.

That was it. I was not allowed to think any more. There was no way rolling back the promise I have made. The research on possible breeds and breeders started. Finally, we decided we would have a Beagle. The sturdy, hyperactive no-nonsense breed. Small enough for the house and loving kind.

Now, we went through various breeders. It was like adopting a child. My daughter joined animal and dog-lovers group on WhatsApp. Finally, we zeroed in on two parties we could get the dog from.

The party nearer home was getting it from Pune. We wanted our pet to come in earlier than what they were promising. The other breeder in Borivali was promising a puppy from Patiala but a lot faster.

Both shared the pictures. Sometimes it felt like we were browsing through a matrimonial site. The breeder sent us photos of the three beagle puppies. The family unanimously liked the pup in the centre, he looked more agile and cute. We did not want to take any chance, we made the advance payment.

Then the wait started. The usual delivery issues got amplified by the day. Every day, we would be promised delivery, and by the evening served excuses why it was getting delayed. It almost came to a stage that we considered asking for the refund of the advance. However, God had other plans, and we were overjoyed when we were told that Beagle was on his way. He had moved from Patiala breeding centre to Delhi, was put on a train, would be collected at Panvel and reach Mumbai soon.

On 11th December we went to the breeder's place in Borivali, and there were the same three puppies we had seen in pictures. It seemed like that. They were so similar that we were confused about which one we had earlier chosen.

We were informed that one of them was already taken. Now between the remaining two, my daughter and I had a unanimous liking for this cute bundle of joy that was still wobbling on his feet. But he was active. He most resembled the one we had earlier seen in the picture.

I planned to name him P3. My son and daughter are nick-named P1 and P2- i.e. Prateek and Preetica. However, Preetica named him Milo. So, Milo Kotnala came home.

So What Happened When Milo Came Home?

Getting a pet home is one thing, but, taking care and bringing him up, as a disciplined member of the family is entirely something different.

In two years since he has been with the family, we can claim to know a lot more of dog psychology. However, what is not a subject of debate is a simple fact. Milo has trained us more than we have taught him.

He has his language of expression. We think we understand him. He is a great theatre artist. He knows what expression gets him what he wants. There is a separate expression for the walk, treat, water, food and such things. We know it and yet like a very gullible person fall for his tricks every time.

Moreover, what is surprising, at least for us is the vocabulary he has gained. He understands simple things like Walk, Goodboy (treat), come, *dischiyoo* (when he rolls as he is shot) etc. We think he even understands whole sentences like, *AC Chalu Kiya, Jao Kamery Mai So Jao* (We have switched on AC, go sleep in the room), *Abhi Time Nahi Hua So Jayo* (Its not yet time for your morning walk, sleep), *Jao P2 Ko Bulao* (Call P2) and a lot more.

Our collective family time has increased. The TV shows other than BiggBoss and India Got Talent have become irrelevant. There is a new baby at home. Everything the family does now revolves around him. For a few months, we even stopped going for movies. His food time is a reality show for the family. The net positivity is up in the family.

MILO CHANGED ME

I was the one who was the only person against getting a pet. Milo is now the centre of my life. I miss him when I travel out of the city on work. Maybe he knows it too. When I return from my frequent trips, the demonstrated love and welcome I get is something only to be experienced. And when I am at home, he is only with me. His unconditional love has changed me.

Earlier, I would not get into a room if there was a pet. Breed and size were immaterial. Now, I welcome the pet company. I have no hesitation in petting any dog. Credit to this transformation goes to Milo Kotnala.

He is everyone's pet. He is extremely friendly and has a huge fan following within the society. Kids adore him. Milo naturally spends maximum time with his Mommy, my wife.

Now, here is the secret, why I finally relented. My daughter most likely will be going to some city for her further education, and we will have an empty-nest. So the youngest kid in the block.

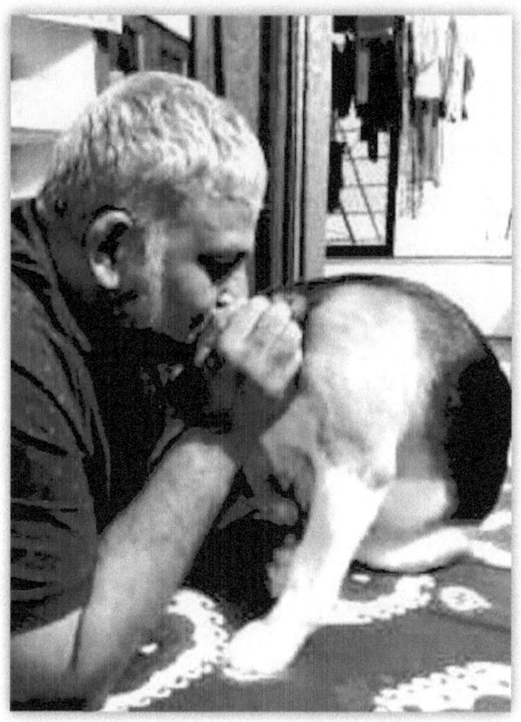

Milo has been with us for exactly two years. And it seems we have been with him for many years. That's the love and affection the family feels. In fact, my son and daughter have a tattoo of his paw mark on their arms.

DON'T BE LATE

I now feel that we were late in getting Milo. Maybe, it was destined that he only joins our family. I urge all families to have a pet. It's a beautiful experience. Additionally, it has the power to create stronger bonds among family members. The children learn a lot by caring for the pet.

I can go on and on. But then it is purely experiential. MILO KOTNALA, thank you for being a part of the family.

SECTION-E
Institute

From IIMA to IIMA

Encounters with the two campuses

Anchal Jain

I grew up in Ahmedabad, the city that housed the mightiest of the IIMs. That is how the city was introduced to us when the family accompanied Dad to visit it the first time, much before actually moving residence from Meerut in the spring of 1976. I was 12 years old.

For me, it was love at first sight with the city that shaped me. The architectural beauty of its public and private buildings captivated me as much as the din of Manek Chowk. My introduction, therefore, to Le Corbusier, came early. I began to sense the influence of brutal architecture and fell in love with it. A lot of it had to do with my school, St. Xavier's Loyola Hall itself, an absolute beauty in contemporary architecture imagined by Hasmukhbhai Patel. I just had to jump walls to land into the hockey field, my eagerness to be enveloped by that campus ensured I was almost always the first to arrive at the school.

Meanwhile, the myth and legend of IIM were even bigger in its host city. It was like this forbidden, out of reach institution where probably sorcery was practised, enhanced by the fact that it was in the ocean of Gujarati enterprise. I had not heard of anyone or their uncles, aunts, cousins, friends or even pets who had been to IIMA. It seemed, IIM belonged to Ahmedabad but not to Amdavadis.

"Don't ever dream of going there", was the code the school abided by. I was no different, not that it mattered to a teenager who was only interested in the sports at the school. There were plenty of them from Pelota (a Basque racquet game) to Baseball and everything in between.

Brother Johnny, a Sunil Gavaskar clone, was God to us. He was also the head coach for almost every sport except Cricket, a game he held in contempt. He would join us for a pre-assembly outing at the Pelota court and also dress a little boy's broken nose at lunchtime basketball. Though I only made to the school hockey team, I was decent at most sports.

However, the game I really loved was the one I never could play well, football. I compensated by becoming the school team mascot, accompanying it to every "away" match in the city. This is how I ended up at the Indian Institute of Management, Ahmedabad.

I did not understand why a school team would be playing a friendly game of football against the giants at IIMA. I was really proud of our team, but as we cycled our way to the campus, we knew we would be roasted that afternoon.

A bunch of 16-year-olds pedalled some twenty minutes through the wilderness to Vastrapur. The IIM campus was quite appropriately set in outskirts of the city to safeguard against any plebeian influence. I do not exaggerate when I say my heart was palpitating as we entered the gates, parked our bicycles and walked to the football pitch. And I was not even playing!

The game was mostly even. We managed to hold the half time score at 0-0. Midway through the second half, something happened. Ahmed Rizwan, my classmate and school captain playing the pivotal midfield role, spotted the goalkeeper off his line. His incredible half-line lob nestled at the back of the IIM net. We rode back not just as victors but also as the slayers of all our demons.

In that flash, Rizwan had shown me that indeed there is no sorcery behind those monstrous brick walls. I was going to conquer this citadel.

When I came to know of my admission at IIMA, I was working in Calcutta. At that moment, the euphoria came from the fact that I will be headed back to Ahmedabad and will be reunited with my college sweetheart, Margie. I had little idea what studying Business Management at IIMA entailed, but it did not matter.

My admission into IIMA did matter actually. A lot. When I got back to Ahmedabad and rang the bell at Margie's. Her mother, who earlier had violently revolted against the idea of her daughter being courted by a "bhaiya" from Uttar Pradesh, hugged me at the door.

The first day at the campus (or the second, even the third) was not as welcoming. It was intimidating, actually. My first brush with life away from home was on the second-floor corner room of a disconcerting red-brick campus. Suddenly "Brutal Architecture" took its literal meaning.

Professor Mote's ominous warning at the opening briefing did not help calm the nerves. "If you can sleep for more than three hours a day, we will think there is something wrong with the programme", he had thundered. I would later quote this line to every new batch at Creative & Cultural Businesses Programme that I ended up Co-Chairing decades later.

He was also the one who finally calmed my nerves, surely against his intentions or even awareness. In the first week at IIM, I discovered every batchmate was distinctly more accomplished, smarter and confident than me. I had begun to doubt if I would last the semester. The first of the infamous MSM quiz, however, saw a good part of the batch score F and Ds. My C+ seemed like a total victory. I struggled to better that score for the rest of the year, but that first quiz from Professor

Mote served to restore my self-belief. Well, enough to defy the "system" and revert to the eight hours of sleep pattern.

The time that was left in the day after the classroom sessions was divided equitably between Margie, case studies and the dorm championships covering Carrom and Cricket. None of them required me to leave the comfort of the second floor at D-10. Trek to the classrooms or the dining hall had started to become a matter of choice. If strategy as I had learnt, was about making choices, I was already a practising manager.

My confined existence at IIMA had consequences. I only knew a few of my batch mates. Only a few knew me. I still loved every moment spent on campus, an iconic design by Louis Kahn. Its intimidating dominance was surprisingly intimate at the same time. It was brutal and beautiful, it was challenging and comforting. Yes, it definitely contributed to the learning, to unforgettable life experience.

Despite very little personal interaction, magically I knew almost the entire batch by name and face. There was a bond, a trust cultivated by the sheer co-existence on this campus for two years. When we dispersed after the convocation, we carried back with us not just the coveted Diploma, but also a bank of indelible memories of shared space and moments with some of the finest minds.

Sadly, as life took over, all this was soon consigned to occasional recollections. Work took me to Paris and beyond for a chunk of the years to follow.

It was in late 2013, a few years after my return to India that I rediscovered my alma mater, this time at the new campus. Like my generation itself, the only IIMA campus I knew was now designated as "Old".

I had heard, of course, that a whole new campus had been built to accommodate the growing needs of the Institute. The intuitive reaction to that was one of scepticism, bordering on revolt. Yet I was inquisitive about how any contemporary architect would stand up against a globally acclaimed, timeless building. My son Utsav had chosen architecture as his career and was already marked for some great work. So, my interest in architecture was even more personal and critical.

When Piyush Sinha, a marketing professor at IIMA, reached out and invited me for an executive programme on luxury management that he was offering, I decided to give it a go.

Luxury was not a domain I professed any expertise, nor did I know what he wanted from me. I was surprised when he asked me if I would help resurrect the programme that was clearly floundering.

I must confess it felt terrific. The idea of being on the "other side" was tempting and daunting at the same time. I had no experience in luxury businesses, none in teaching or research. I had not kept up with the latest in management science either. I had been an entrepreneur all my life, more of an intuition person than rigorously rational.

The temptation of teaching and running a programme at IIMA quickly trumped my fears and insecurities. However, when Piyush introduced me to the programme details, I began to lose my interest.

"Why do we need to teach Indian professionals to think for and like a Gucci or a Louis Vuitton?" I asked him. He just asked me to sleep over it and suggest what I would like to do instead.

"Meanwhile, I have a Retail Management course for PGPX students. Would you like to take a couple of sessions on online retail?" I picked a case on "Tao Bao" with no idea what I will do in the class for 150 minutes to keep the students from walking out.

Shrikant Gokhale, my batchmate and a veteran at it already, argued that if he could teach just anyone could. Somehow, I believed the founding member of Pleasure Inc at IIMA '85.

I wonder when we got admitted to IIMA did we sign up for a minimum number of classes to attend. And, if we do not complete the quota before passing out, must we come back to teach.

Meanwhile, the new campus captivated me. The rendition in exposed concrete captured the essence of Louis Kahn and yet made a strikingly different statement. A move on, yet a very respectful one.

A bigger surprise came from discovering the name of the architect; Bimal Patel. He had the twin task of delivering on the challenge posed by Louis Kahn as well as stand up as a worthy successor to the practice started by Hamukhbhai, his father. Hasmukhbhai, who decades earlier, had designed my school. The loop was indeed closed, and there was a strange joy in that.

Shrikant was co-teaching the course on retail management with Piyush. As the three of us walked to the classroom, I was overcome with fearful anticipation. "The only thing I can envision right now is the authority that our professors commanded when they were in the well of the classroom. I have none of that, how the hell am I going to survive?" I asked Piyush and Shrikant.

The answer was stunning. "Do you also recall what you felt when you were seated in the class in 1986? The students you are going to teach will be no different. They will believe your authority unless you give them a reason to think otherwise."

The class passed off as any first attempt would, I thought I was okay, not great. As we stepped out, I asked Piyush and Shrikant, how they felt it went. Piyush was again philosophical, "Did you feel good, because that is all that matters".

I don't know about good, I admittedly felt relieved. Later Piyush was to give me a handy and obvious tip, "you are good with the case, and you will be great when you can also leave the students with academic learning."

Until now, I had not been able to give much attention or thought to the Luxury Programme. But now I wanted to do it, come back to the classroom and do really well. Make my second life at IIMA count more than my first.

I stayed up all night, my first at the new campus, and began to think about the executive programme afresh. Forget the luxury bit, I told myself, and think about what and why you would want to do a programme at IIMA.

I always felt that while western consumers were ready for Indian products and brands, we Indians were not. This was more palpable in creative and lifestyle domain where aesthetics played a key role. While India had centuries-old skills to offer, we were still left wondering what to do with both crafts and craftsmen. I had been witnessing more and more of young and ambitious creative talent emerging in the country, a lot of them were driven by the notion of inclusive entrepreneurship. I was convinced that a few days of intervention would not change anything in the current eco-system. The programme must have a more in-depth and more extended connection with the participants.

Next day, I presented my blueprint for a new programme, focusing on lifestyle and creative entrepreneurs and harnessing the Indian Heritage for the world. It would run for about five months, with entrepreneurs coming together for fifteen days over three camps. It would be expensive to deliver, but I was convinced of its value to participants.

Piyush told me to present it to the then Director, Ashish Nanda, who would have to authorize it. My pitch was quite simple, "Just as we need not be afraid of the global influence on our lifestyle, we should not be shy of influencing the world. We can do that if we equip a whole crop of creatively skilled entrepreneurs with business and branding principles. If we succeed, we would have done a great service to the non-farm rural economy as well, as there lies the richness that the world awaits".

"Let's do it" were his immediate words.

I don't think I had invested so much of myself in anything I have done so far. It felt different. The programme was not to make money for a start but to share and nurture. The responsibility suddenly felt infinitely more.

To teach, I had to learn, which I did, probably far more than I did at the old campus. I wanted to be in the classroom all the time, it became an addiction. Every time I finished a class, I wanted to start it again and do it better. When I look back at the seven years, I cannot recognize my early sessions, convinced that there is still more to share the next time.

Yet, the programme was not just about taking a few sessions. It was even more about influencing the direction that many young entrepreneurs would take. Every session, mine or otherwise, would need to add up to a larger whole and make a strong impact. I needed help, and I found that in Geetanjali.

I stole her from New York, where she was working with Gucci. Driven by a shared vision, she accepted to work part-time on an RA's stipend of Rs 30,000 a month. She was the kind I wanted in the class. At Crafting Luxury and Lifestyle Businesses (as it was called at inception), she was the one most suited to critically audit the programme's content. She also took on the responsibility of marketing it to others like her.

She took her role very seriously. She became our most challenging customer, the gatekeeper of the programme who would demand improvements to enhance the participants' experience. By the end of 2017, five batches later, it was already attracting five to six times more applications than the accepted intake.

It got the attention of the industry in India and abroad as well. The valedictory ceremony in itself became an event to remember, with well-known names in creative firmament joining us in celebrating the journeys of the participants.

Meanwhile, I was clueless about how the internal administration at IIMA worked. Piyush dealt with that, and I had no reason to think about it. Or so I thought.

We had finished the fifth valedictory on a high. Ermenegildo Zegna of the eponymous brand stated categorically, "Luxury brands can only be built by families". Being a third-generation head of the world's largest men's luxury brand, his words carried substance, and they rang truthfully.

Next morning, however, was quite different. Piyush met me before I left campus and told me that he would probably need to quit. He warned that the programme would most likely be shut down. The circumstances made his departure from IIMA quite sure. CLLB was going to be collateral damage. A couple of weeks later, I got forwarded email saying that the programme shall henceforth not be offered.

While I had nothing to lose from a financial standpoint, the disappointment and anger refused to leave me.

Doing this programme had been meditative for me, emotional experience of sharing and giving with no expectation of returns. Yet it gave me a lot, a sense of being, an identity. The participants hated me, and they loved me. An extraordinary surge of support and alternative hosting offers poured in from friends, academia, industry and above all, the CLLB alumni.

I remember our 31st batch reunion at Udaipur in February 2018, a few weeks after the CLLB shut down. One afternoon

Janat Shah, who went on to be the first Director at IIM Udaipur, hosted us all at his beautiful IIM Udaipur campus.

Some thirty of us were sharing our life journeys. I went last, and this is how I started. "Listening to all of you wind down and almost retire makes me wonder if I have lost my last 30 years because I am just getting started". Indeed, CLLB had got me started on a new journey, I was just discovering myself.

I wasn't walking away. I resolved not to give up the vision, with or without IIMA.

While I evaluated options, I found a sympathizer at IIM in Prof Rakesh Basant, Dean for Alumni Affairs. He told me he would try to ask Prof Errol D'Souza, the new Director, to talk to me. That's all, there was no further promise. There was another believer in the programme, Prof Amit Karna. He agreed to Co-Chair the programme with me in the event it got the approval.

The meeting with Errol lasted ten minutes.

Director Errol began by apologizing for not speaking with me earlier, explaining that he had no idea I was involved so deeply in the programme. While that left me perplexed, given the circumstances, I could understand. I briefly told him about the vision, and the journey traversed thus far, adding that I am certainly not pausing. Also, as Amit was already on board, he agreed to give it a go.

Amit and I struck a great partnership. As this story gets published, two fresh batches would have gone through the new avatar of CLLB, rechristened and restructured as "Creative and Cultural Businesses Programme" (CCBP).

Reflecting back on the turn of events, I have no hesitation in saying that CCBP is clearly a more robust, complete rendition. While we can undoubtedly call it a happy success, we have miles to travel still. A few thousand actually, before the programme makes it mark internationally.

No Alternative No Problem

Sanjeev Kotnala

"No Alternative. No Problem". I love it. It is one thing I learnt at IIM Ahmedabad. I regularly use it in my workshops. It has been drilled, and yes, it is such a potent debate doubt closure.

When you have no alternatives to choose from, there is no problem.

A problem has to do with alternative solutions. Just like a lock must have a key; otherwise, the lock is just a paperweight. It is everything but a lock.

It is possible, you may not have a solution right now, but the alternatives do exist even in the most constrained ecosystem.

Class of 1987 gives Prof. V. L. Mote the credit for the statement 'When You Don't Have An Alternative, You Don't Have A Problem'. The class of 1987, IIM Ahmedabad believes, Prof Mote, voiced this gem of knowledge while teaching decision tree in the first year. The debate is still on as to when did Prof V.L. Mote said the famous line? What did he precisely say? And what he exactly meant?

Sadly we can't check it with him, as our dear respected Prof V.L. Mote recently passed away on the way to attaining Nirvana.

The No Alternative No Problem Guru

Prof. Mote passing away, created a hyper debate in IIMA groups on WhatsApp. The Class of 1987 was no different. His profound Jeevan mantra was discussed in the university of WhatsApp.

The debate helped me correct and sharpen my understanding. I realized I may have misunderstood the mantra, all this time. The discussion, as expected, was sharp. These were anyway a set of people with a strong mindset.

Someone in the group had to remind the people not to take the debate seriously. Another batchmate almost shouted, 'Chill! Chill! You are no MBA. Just PGDM."

Applying The Filters

Now Prof Mote was an extraordinary professor. He was one of the founding professors at IIMA who has taught many industry stalwarts. He gave us one of the best fundas for life, "If You Don't Have An Alternative, You Don't Have A Problem".

Yes, I know everyone may not accept it, and that is expected. So, I was not surprised when one of the Gyani's (GYANI-I) in the group differed. He countered, "If you do not have an alternative, you do not have a solution. You certainly still have a problem". The shout was loud and clear, and there was not much debate that it made sense. Another pious soul (PIOUS SOUL) interrupted. He questioned if Prof Mote really did say, "no alternative. No Problem. Is Nirvana".

Bringing You The Debate On Alternative

The IIMA87 group is reasonably active. Each one is sensitive about how they are perceived. There is a free for all for everyone to work on their Brand-i. They discuss global issues for breakfast. Today, they considered, President Trump freak 'Mr Modi asked me to mediate' statement, and how in a good economy he can be easily be re-elected. Nearer home, they deliberated on Urjit Patel, pointing out what is wrong with banking. But, the most engaging discussion was on Prof Mote's mantra. It has been a tough task to read through hundreds of screens and cryptic clues. However, this can be considered a reasonably well-articulated synopsis.

Listening To Alternate Point-Of-Views

We have a lady (LADY) in the group who thinks differently. She is the Gaurav of the group. We pride ourselves that within us is she who never argues without supporting her point of view with data points and well-researched information.

She has facts for every argument she supports. The not so young Lady can beat anyone in and outside the group in a debate on any subject. She has strong views and a perfect way to present them.

The Lady said "Prof Mote fundas need to be seen contextually. He asked a question, What's the problem? And he was referring to the case. What are the solution alternatives? If it's only one alternative as a solution, then there is no problem. There is no decision making or evaluation involved. The only solution is a state of Nirvana. It is my understanding of what Prof Mote said, so many times."

Finally, the penny dropped for me. I have been missing this crucial bridge. I tend to agree with her. And agreeing with her is anyway most of the time a good strategy.

The Debate On Alternatives And Problem Picks Up

You can't allow someone else's points of view to win so easily. Not when the bricks of IIM Ahmedabad have influenced you, and you are expert in raising counter-arguments. Some times just for the fun of it. Some times seriously protecting your Brand-I. Sometimes, such discussion in the WhatsApp group adds to the group's collective learning.

So the GYANI-I politely disagreed with the argument. He pointed out, "for example if I am a homeless person and do not have money to rent or buy a shelter. And if there are no homeless shelters. Then, I may not have any alternatives and hence, no solution! Being homeless is a problem for me, and lack of alternatives does not prevent it from being a problem. Just because I cannot escape homelessness, it does not make it a state of Nirvana.'

I understand there are always alternatives. Status quo itself is an alternative. But, I liked Gyani-I's argument.

I smiled when the Lady went for the kill. "There are still 'alternatives', albeit ones that may not meet your' objectives,' e.g., sleeping on the footpath, out on streets, forceful break-in and more."

Maybe she did get it wrong this time. Gyani-I was not going to give up so quickly, "Sleeping on the footpath and out on the street is NOT an alternative to homelessness!"

The Lady relented a bit. She paraphrased her argument again; she said "Prof Mote said that, but I disagree. If you do not have an alternative, you do not have a solution. You certainly can still have a problem. And if Prof Mote said "If you have no alternative you are in a state of Nirvana" because you have no decision-making problem. I agree. However, it does not mean "you have no problem".

Wow, I was getting re-educated.

The Alternatives

The vagabond guru (VG) chipped in. "When Mote spoke about alternatives, pretty sure he was talking about legal alternatives and so forceful break-in does not qualify."

A section of group uninterested in this academic debate wanted to leave the Professor in peace and stop the discussion. There were alternatives before the group. They could continue the conversation, stop it, take it one-on-one or open a new WhatsApp group for people interested in the debate.

Thankfully, before the group could engage in democratic debate on what to do, some said 'Managerial Problems is always about the problem of choice', and it reignited the discussion.

Gyani-I was still stuck at Nirvana, so he added "I do not agree with Nirvana. Just because one does not have a decision-making problem, does not mean he or she is at Nirvana. In the homeless example, I may not have alternatives and hence, no solution. Being homeless is a problem for me, and lack of alternatives does not prevent it from being so.'

The academician (ACAD) in the group jumped in with a fresh perspective. "See, This person's problem is not homelessness, but pennilessness. Surely there are alternative solutions to that as a problem. I do agree with what Prof. Mote said. No alternatives do mean there is no decision to make and instead one should focus on something else".

It seems someone in the group had his fundas right.

Gyani Rises To The challenge With Alternative Thinking

Gyani-I felt challenged with the way the discussion was shaping up. He pointed out, "I agree no alternatives mean no decision to make. I am responding to the comment that no alternatives mean no problem. I also agree one should focus on something else, but that is hardly Nirvana. Additionally, a homeless person may not be broke. He may have money for food but not for a home. So cannot say the problem is not homelessness but pennilessness".

The Lady decided to hedge her bets as the discussion was going no-where. "Did Prof Mote say, "No alternatives means there is no decision making and hence focus on something else'. If he said it, I have no alternative but to agree. However, If Prof Mote said "If you don't have an alternative then you don't have a problem', I disagree with that. I have not heard him directly so depending on what he said, I either agree or disagree".

I now understand why she always wins an argument.

Absolute Take On Alternative And Problems

"If you have alternatives, you have a problem. If you don't have alternatives, you are well and truly F****D!"

Then the one who now lives innovating carpentering lives (ICL) in western India broke the rule. He reminded the Lady. "Yes, Prof Mote did teach section-A, your section. Remember, Prof Mote took the Western India pharmaceuticals case. He threw duster at me! Maybe it was the introduction to the case method, but definitely, it was section A".

He quoted Prof Mote' if there are no alternatives, you do not have a decision problem. There is no mention of the problem vanishing. It is in the context of the decision trees. There, If you don't have alternatives, you are in a state of Nirvana. You have only one path to follow. It does not say that the problem ceases to exist. It suggests you don't have any choice but to follow the only solution on hand."

The above explanation sounded conclusive enough. However, I am surprised at people remembering the cases they discussed in the early eighties. Throwing the duster was irrefutable proof from Section A. The discussion should stop.

The Lady further made her point, "I very clearly remember what Prof Mote said. If you don't have any alternative, you are in a state of Nirvana. Then he explained that it means you have only one path to follow. It does not mean that you can do something else or that you don't have a problem. It only means that you have no choice but to follow that single path".

Discussion Thrives On Alternatives

Another Gyani (Gyani-II) woke up to provide his input to the discussion. "If you don't have a problem, and don't have alternatives, you have achieved Nirvana". And in an authentic style added, "Time to draw a two by two. The problem, no problem, on the x-axis. Alternatives, no alternatives, on the Y-axis." And I started thinking about what quadrant would be 'No Problem. Many Alternatives'.

A Bird (BIRD) who keeps coming in and out of discussions chirped in "I think we should write a case study on this and develop a model. It is sure an HBR material. We can draw on the fields of psychology, epistemology, game theory, logic, sociology, and python programming".

I noted, the group still holds HBR in high esteem. Maybe the 'H' hangover remains.

Alternative Leading To Nirvana Gets Interesting

Now the IIMA Alumni can never allow a discussion to just fizzle out. Habits don't die so quickly. So the promotors of the homeless angle brought it back. "Not escaping homelessness is still a sense of Nirvana. Once you recognize, there is no way to solve a problem. It will merely unmask the problem. No decision or cause for exercising free will and the unhappiness associated with choice. Nirvana will descend. Decision making among choice is the root of all problems, symbolized by Adam's apple". I did not understand the last part, but I let that go.

The ex-academician (EXA) who till now was having a ring-side, jumped in and suggested that Prof Mote actually said something different. According to EXA he said 'If you have no alternative you are in a state of Nirvana' because you have no decision-making problem'. And that does not mean 'you have no problem'. No one had time to remind him. It has been discussed before.

The EXA made the ultimate CP. "If you have alternatives, you have a problem. If you don't have alternatives, you are well and truly F****D! being well and genuinely F****D is Nirvana."

Closing The Alternative Gap

The initial propagator of the discussion Gyani-I was openly feeling ill at ease. He fired his last shot. "Just saying the situation without any alternatives is Nirvana. You can't do shit about the situation, so accept it. It will help one make decisions on the next goal and the path to take. One can't be in a defeatist mode. Apologies if I started something."

The person from Allahabad (PFA) shot in like the hot iron, "You guys are talking about acceptance as if it is as easy as flicking a switch. So click, and Nirvana appears. There is no sensible alternative to live in. So every living being is in a state of Nirvana? Did you ever have a situation in life did you accept totally without any questions? The journey to real acceptance goes through hell. Because the barriers to real acceptance are your cravings and aversions, and it is difficult to eliminate them fully. Yes, you can mask them by playing tricks with your brain, but they do not become extinct and resurface stronger at the right time. So what's the alternative?"

The batch of 1987 has to feel its age. So the Gyani-III in the group had to remind them. "The alternative at this age and stage in life is gradual renunciation. Those hurdles go poof. Nirvana appears. As you say, renunciation seems like "going thru hell. If it is forced."".

A rebuttal to it came immediately. 'What you are saying is true. If you understand you are not renouncing, but with age, gradually your desires and aversions are running out of fuel.'

Howlers @ 99.Percentile

Dilip Thosar

Halcyon days, the first week of our immigration and habitation in the hallowed precincts of IIMA. Later we learnt that we should call it WIMWI – Well-known Institute of Management in Western India, not IIMA: the latter was for the awe-filled hoi-polloi who couldn't make it in. Almost half the batch seemed to be engineers and with work experience. So, we were expecting the usual welcome ragging, and because it was simply invisible, wondering when, and in what form, which monster will pounce on us. But the hubris of having entered the golden gates of competitive heaven sustained with no interruption.

On day 1 (if I remember right, it was in June 1985), our director Prof.N.R.Sheth made a welcome speech to us in the sacred space of WIMWI: the Louis Kahn Plaza. On our right was the wing of the classes showing off its bare bricks. On our left was the wing with offices for the teaching staff, and the library majestically rose in front, on the green manicured lawns of the LKP. Among things he said, one thing stuck in my mind as a "Fevicol jod".

He said, "…*each of you is the crème de la crème where you come from. All 180 of you are among the absolutely top percentile talent of the nation. You have topped brilliantly right through your academic term and breezed through the CAT and the tough interview process. You are undoubtedly the very best.*"

With a pause for impact, he swooped for the kill "*Now I want you to get ready for a surprise that may hit you if you are not prepared. Your performance here will be graded, and someone will come tops while someone inevitably will be ranked 180th, the bottomer of the class! And half of you toppers will suddenly see yourself in the bottom 50 percentile half of the class, down from the 99 you are used to! A few of you would see yourselves inched out of the race for the gold medal by the proverbial line of split hair. So, be ready for this and don't let it be a nasty surprise anymore. Do not see your middling rank as a failure*".

It was an impressive warning, helped carry me through the 2-year super-grind and digest the inevitable "failures" of "middling ranks" there with ease.

In the first week at IIMA, we got a notice by word-of-mouth that our seniors (2nd-year gods) have arranged a special show of the world-famous play "Amadeus" for our batch. The venue was equally famous Tagore Hall near the heart of the city (Ahmedabad), and those of us who don't land up are undoubtedly going to miss a significant event in their lives. So the newly knighted competitive supermen and superwomen of this country, immediately after classes, got onto the march. What did we know that we were not the knighted ones but the benighted ones! Very anxious, we packed in twos and threes. Some in autorickshaws. Many taking lifts from locals who had cars or two-wheelers. And a few sportsmen even walking the few kilometres through unknown ghettos, we reached the hall. There we saw something unexpected. A group of our seniors near the gates. What were they doing there? Cajoling and directing us in and of a bunch of our batchmates muttering under their breath, discussing whether they should return to campus. Undaunted and still haunted by the Almighty Competitive Spirit, we pushed further through the crowd, to grab the best seats in the hall.

As we went in, we found the doors locked. Oh God, were we late, would we now be forced to forego the great opportunity our seniors gave us? That was when some seniors, with a loud guffaw, let us in on the secret: there was no Play, just a prank being played by their batch onto ours. Chafing at the realization that the pursuit of success had made us highly competitive and paranoid. We grabbed anything that was touted as an opportunity, we soberly quietly and quickly returned to the campus. By the time we reached our dorms, the frowns had turned to smiles. It dawned upon our hyperactive wily brains that every dog would have his day, "Apna bhi time aayega".

Our seniors had also passed on some good legacy to us, in particular a weekly ragmag called "Synchrony" handed down by four crazy guys among the seniors to five crazy guys in our batch: Sundaram Sundy (among the youngest of the batch and a mega-marathoner in US at 55), Kapil Kapoor KK (later Chairman Timex India), Ajay Srinivasan, one among the few all-rounders in the batch (later CEO Aditya Birla Capital) and Girish Phatarphod (the zaniest genius in the batch) and me.

The content of Synchrony was crack stuff about local events, created on Sunday early mornings (after completing the project assignments till 2 AM) by the editors. The editors would hand-craft on the template paper and get it cyclostyled in the institute machine. The same machine, which was otherwise used to cyclostyle the case-material for students.

The heap of cyclostyled sheets would be carried personally by editors to the mess, to be consumed by the masses over the special breakfast dosas on Sunday mornings. The "editors" sat in the IIMA mess from opening till closing time, looking on hungrily, as any artist would, for the smiles and guffaws breaking out on the faces of readers.

As part of the activities of Synchrony, we took upon ourselves to get the "apnaa time" to come ASAP. After our summer internships, we returned to campus for the second year, a maturing career-focused bunch, their competitive spirit further sharpened by the first year and the internships. The first years looked like we were seeing a mirror that showed us a year ago. We missed and remembered the PGP-IIIs. The 'departed souls' who would surely return someday to haunt and humour us with, among other things, crates of highly desirable spirits that were officially banned in the dry state. That's when, we, the Synchrony cronies took upon ourselves the noble duty of passing on the hallowed tradition of the annual prank to the newly inducted juniors – PGP-Is,. And of course, with more panache and culture than what we got from the now-PGP3s.

Our first-year darshan of the hyper-competitive placement orientation of the institute gave us the idea for the prank. We got one of the faculty members to join our conspiracy. He signed the notice, inviting the fresher batches, for a very special lecture by Prof. Dr Venkataramaiah from Harvard Business School (the role model for WIMWI).

Posters were put up. We also got approval for us to use classroom CR324 as the venue. Birdie, aka S. Nagnath (who went on to head DSP Merrill Lynch / Blackrock), was our unanimous choice to personify Dr Venkatramaiah. He had an incredible talent of punching out the weirdest lines, dripping with management jargon, all the while keeping the most poker-faced countenance one can imagine.

We made it a point to let the freshers know that we have taken special permission from the director to allow them to attend the function that was meant for the next batch. Simply because we did not them want to miss the rare golden opportunity of hearing "Dr Venkatramaiah himself" at such close-quarters.

Our batchmates were there too, ostensibly to not miss the opportunity but really, obviously, to enjoy the glee of watching the faces of juniors during and after the show. We, the Synchrony board, were the hosts of dis(honour), trying to match Birdie's straight countenance.

Birdie, oops, Dr Venkatramaiah, entered the auditorium dressed in a baggy oversized grey chequered tweed coat with a matching greying moustache stuck on his smooth under-nose, to thunderous applause from the freshers (of course, seeded by some of our batchmates in there).

Birdie was welcomed by Ramki, our batchmate playing the role of MC. Ramki announced in that typical awe-oozing way that student MCs introduce giant-profiled speakers to the audience. Dr Venkatramaiah's rags-to-riches propelled-by-geewiz-smartness story replete with life sketch. "Dr Venkatramaiah grew up in a small village called Tadepalligudam in Andhra Pradesh, studied in a Telugu medium Government school. After spending a couple of months at IIMA as an invited platinum-level faculty, Dr Venkatramaiah migrated to the US on an invitation from Harvard to be a tenured professor. His claim to fame, his famous theory of "Personality Metamorphosis" and is in town on a consulting assignment for the Gujarat Government. Concluding his prepared and doctored speech, Ramki invited the learned professor to take the stage and explain and demonstrate his grand theory.

Birdie too kept up the façade with his quintessential poker-face and spoke some very high-sounding meaningless management jargon. We watched with unabashed glee the faces of the juniors sitting in rapt attention. Mostly dressed in full formals (grin!), all sincerely trying to impress the awesome wise speaker. CP in hushed tones was heard: "Wow, he's from Harvard. He's got such a hep accent but still maintains his Telugu roots". After a brief two minutes speech, some of the hyper-competitive superstars even asked him some questions. They used equally high-sounding jargon, about management, career and the possibility of them cosying up to him so he could recommend them to some exceptional placement opportunities. "Do you think Sir, after our MBA here, we should do another MBA at Harvard?", "Technology is rapidly developing. Do you think we MBAs will get obsolete"?" "Sir, what according to you is the role of intrapreneurship in management?" He even promised to "see what he could do there". This part of the show was humongously hilarious, but we kept our traps shut, smothering all indications of unholy mirth.

Finally, a mole in the audience asked the planted question. It was the last permissible one, "Sir, can you enlighten us about how individuals and organizations can metamorphose their personalities, hopefully with the promised demo please"? With a grand wave of his hands, Dr Venkataramaiah declared that he would now demonstrate his specialization miracle of how to implement "Personality Metamorphosis". Saying so, Birdie removed his baggy coat. He pulled out a handkerchief from his pocket, dipped it in the glass of water on the podium and slowly rubbed it to unglue his moustache. He concluded in his jargon rich way of speaking, which has unfortunately been lost to history. Dear students, this is how one morphs one's personality, from the highly acclaimed Dr.Venkataramaiah to a second-year student at WIMWI. Before the first-year students could recover from the shock and lynch him, he ran for cover in the security of his batchmates crowding outside the door.

So two years flew by, and all of us entered the corporate world at the promised fourth step on the fast elevator. Entrepreneurship wasn't the fashion, let alone a passion, those days. We would wallow in the pleasure of good fortune when folks would look at us with awe the moment they heard we were ex-IIMA. We indulged in this unabashed narcissistic hedonism.

As the decades flew by, some of our batchmates became really big figures. Especially in the last few years, we experienced a peculiar déjà vu in every group or party we were ever part of. I, like many of us, would invoke immense awe in any party, if one let it slip by that, say, Raghuram Rajan was my batchmate at IIMA! And then sometimes it was Harish Bhat or Phaneesh Murthy, and then few others, who wielded pretty high-profile corporate positions and social visibility. MDs and CEOs of companies.

We happily sloshed around in the name-dropping game, till the backlash started hitting. Someone would say in great awe, "Wow, you are Raghuram Rajan's batchmate!" skyrocketing me to a stellar position in the motley group. Then after a short pause, would come the inevitable question, "Wow! Hmm. So,… what do YOU do"? Dunking us into the ground from the dizzy heights with double the speed. As a natural corollary to claiming to be a buddy of these great figures, we would obviously be expected to also have reached similar heights professionally. Obviously, most of us hadn't.

I remembered the wise words of our director's first-day speech, whose wisdom proved way beyond campus life. I would mumble out some nice eulogy about my current activities and sheepishly try to turn the conversation elsewhere. Like all of us, I am a resolute lifelong learner.

Recently I learnt from an IIMC friend, a wonderful counter-measure to this significant rise and fall syndrome. Decades after leaving campus, he too used to be embarrassed by the same awful awe-fall. After a few tries of "well, I manage logistics for xxx ltd for the Asia Pacific" or some like that, he built an excellent answer to that devastating question "So, what do YOU do"? He would render the curious querier stunned and speechless by replying with a sincere stone face: "Me? I attend weddings of sons and daughters of my batchmates. Well, what do YOU do?

Contributing Authors

Class of '87, IIM AHMEDABAD

Prof A G Balasubramanian

Prof A G Balasubramanian (b 1959) is a retired professor and presently resides in Kochi. He did his doctoral programme (FPM) at IIM during 1985-89. He spent almost his entire career as a business school professor in several schools and about half of it was at Goa Institute of Management. He presently spends his time reading, occasionally teaching and sometimes writing. He can be contacted at agbalasubramanian@yahoo.com

Ankur Mittal

Ankur Mittal is a professional with a wide variety of experiences at work. From a banker at the start of his working life, to being a BPO professional, to becoming an entrepreneur and founding businesses in the HR Tech space, and now working for an organisation in the social space, he embodies the 'change is the only constant' philosophy. Along the way, he rediscovered his interest in writing and has published two books. He supports environmental conservation through his efforts at consuming less.

Anchal Jain

Anchal has 32 years of entrepreneurial, advisory and academic experience in creative and lifestyle industries. He was the founder and CEO of Primetex Sarl based in Paris. In his career, he has participated very closely in complete value chain management in fashion and lifestyle businesses, including trend forecasting and data analytics.

In 2013, IIM Ahmedabad invited him to serve as the Co-Chair at Creative & Cultural Businesses Programme (CCBP), now a benchmark programme in creative and lifestyle entrepreneurial learning in India.

Anchal is a thought leader in Artisanal Renaissance in India, including reflections on Indianness and its power in global markets, sustainability, integral entrepreneurship and value creation at the grassroots level.

He is a member of 'FICCI Skills Development Committee' and 'Task Force on Cluster-based model of job creation'.

He is one of the founding partners at Val-More Action Advisory, a holistic end-to-end business solution for Lifestyle, FMCG and Healthcare businesses using its proprietary business output based framework focusing on four pillars viz. Value Creation Strategy, Golden Thread Execution, Knowledge Transfer & Capability Building and Value-Based Funding.

Chiranjeev Kohli

Chiranjeev Kohli holds a Ph.D. in Marketing from Indiana University. His dissertation received honorable mention in the *International Doctoral Dissertation Competition*. As a Professor of Marketing at California State University Fullerton, he was honored with the Business School's Best Professor Award twice, and by the Young Presidents Organization of Southern California for excellence in academia.

He also received the Best Professor Award from the University's Associated Students. In addition, he has won several other research and teaching awards. Dr. Kohli's research has been reported in leading academic journals and media outlets, including *Harvard Business Review* and *National Public Radio*.

Dr. Kohli is the founder principal of I.D.ENTITY, specializing in brand and corporate identity. He has consulted for companies such as *Alcatel Lucent, Autodesk, Canon USA, Spherion, Taco Bell,* and *Verizon.* He has offered several seminars in the United States, Germany, Hong Kong, India, Sweden, and Vietnam. A comedian by avocation, he won the Indiana University Comedy Competition and has opened for Dennis Miller of *Saturday Night Live*! He can be reached at 714.770.0250 or ckohli@identitypulse.com

Dilip Thosar

Dilip claims to learn about human life and ways, working in diverse environments: own ventures, with startups, with multinational corporations.

He showed certain proclivities in creativity and STEM and looks forward to now pass these on to the nextgen so at least they may use these.

He has been fortunate to be exposed to and inspired by great people, including batchmates at IIMA.

At this time, he is upping his ante in Business Analytics and Machine Learning, hoping to work towards understanding Real Intelligence

Girish Phatarphode

Girish Phatarphode worked with ICICI for 5 years after doing Post-Graduation from IIM, Ahmedabad in 1987. Once, disenchanted with the corporate life, he turned independent consultant. Since then he has been helping corporates in making numbers speak- see patterns- and he is an avid painter and a storyteller.

Giri

Over the years, Giri has built a broadbased career - across multiple businesses - consumer businesses, financial services, retail and pharma - and across multiple geographies - Asia and Europe. Has lived and worked in India, Dubai, Singapore and London.Giri loves to build high performance teams.

He has significant experience in business and financial transformation. He has won several CFO awards. He is a Founding Member of the CFO Board (www.cfoboard.com) which consists of the senior most CFOs in the country acting as a thinktank for providing non-partisan points of view on key policy issues to the Government, the Ministry of Finance in particular.

He is deeply passionate about Authentic Leadership and committed to Doing Well by Doing Good. It may be noted that Giri is a Trustee of the Taj Public Service Welfare Trust, whose purpose is to reach out to people affected by disasters, both man-made and natural, with support to rebuild their lives.

Gyaneshwar Tripathi

Gyaneshwar Tripathi, better known as Trips, is an engineer from IIT BHU and a Post-Graduate from IIMA.

He has 32 years of leadership experience in large Industrial companies in GC Cana Africa.

He started his career in Finance with a good stint with ICICI and in 1998 moved to Bank Muscat, Oman as VP – Project Finance & Investment Banking.

In 2001, Trips moved over to corporate side as COO of a large manufacturing Group in Dubai. In 3 years, he successfully turned around the Group into a profitable group.

Trips moved to higher profile roles from 2007 and since then has held Board level positions of Group CFO for two large Industrial Groups in UAE engaged in steel, electrical equipment, cement and polymer manufacturing. He was instrumental in establishing and managing Steel & other industrial companies and executing large M&A transactions in GCC and Africa.

He spent 18 years in COO/ Group CFO/ acting CEO roles working at Board levels and being accountable for the P&L and shareholder value creation.

He has considerable experience in establishing, operating and divesting manufacturing companies in GCC & Africa and is considered an expert on this subject for GCC & Africa.

Kumar Ekambaram

E. Kumar (Kumar Ekambaram) brings with him about 39 years of work experience in multiple sectors and work cultures. He is an electrical engineer and a management graduate from IIM Ahmedabad. He has worked in Dairy, Packaging, Healthcare, Hospitality, Telecom, Realty and ITES sectors across India, setting up business ventures from grassroots and growing the business and team.

The organisations he has worked for, ranges from large corporate groups to global Private-equity managed ventures. He started as trainee engineer with National Dairy Development Board setting milk chilling centres and aseptic Milk Packaging Station across India.

After 5 years quit and joined IIM A to pursue Post Graduate Diploma in Management. After passing out of IIM A, worked for Apollo Hospitals Group setting up Hospitals across the country and after 7 years moved to Tata Group.

In Tata Group he set up Hotels for Taj Group and then moved to Tata Teleservices to roll out CDMA telecom network. While with the group set up a BPO for Tata Group to cater to domestic market. After 14 years with Tata Group he moved to work for Venture Capitalists Funds in the realty and ITES sector. Finally in 2013 moved out of corporate sector and now is an independent management consultant and a certified CEO Coach.

N. Subramaniam

N. Subramaniam is Son of an Indian Railways Officer who grew up mostly in South India. He was already a qualified CA and Cost Accountant when he took admission at IIM Ahmedabad and was in two minds to take it up. His parents encouraged him as it was a prestigious portal of learning and they could afford the fee since his dad was still in service.

He worked with Hindustan Aeronautics and ICI (Imperial Chemical Industries) now Akzo Nobel before he came to IIM Ahmedabad. After graduating, he joined the Bank of America and was privileged to be part of the new Treasury, Forex and Investment division, where he spent 7 years in two stints. It was unusual in those days to leave a Bank and come back to work in the same organization, which has become rather normal in IT services today.

He moved from Banking to Equity investments in 1995 to set up a private sector Mutual Fund and graduated to Private Equity in 1997 where he have spent 20 years to retire in 2017. He currently sit on Boards of Listed Companies as Independent Director, notable among them is City Union Bank (CUB) a Tamil Nadu based small regional Bank. He is associated with charitable causes across Old Age homes, Support for mental health patients, Paediatric Heart surgeries, etc.

He is now focusing in finding and developing hobbies since retirement and making a serious attempt to be a part of celebrations with friends and family, sharing joy full time.

He can be reached at : mcapsubbu@gmail.com

Rajiv Kakar

Rajeev Kakar is a graduate of IIT Delhi (1985) and IIM Ahmedabad (1987). Post his MBA he started a career in banking and worked with Citibank for the first two decades of his career. In 2006, he Cofounded Fullerton Financial Holdings headquartered in Singapore (the global Banking and Financial services arm of Temasek Holding) to focus on building and operating banks and FIs, across multiple emerging markets.

He is a seasoned banker, business founder, entrepreneur, and Corporate Board Member with over three decades of global banking experience and expertise in financial services, especially in Emerging Local Corporate / Commercial / MSME / Retail Banking, across high-growth emerging markets in the Asia Pacific/China, Europe, Indian Sub-Continent, MENA/ GCC, and Central/Eastern Europe regions.

He has a strong track record of successfully operating large banks/financial institutions, leading business turnarounds with a demonstrated ability to conceptualize and execute multi-country business strategies, leading acquisitions and business/ digital transformations, launching green-field financial services businesses, delivering profitability over a sustained period while contributing to the community. He currently serves on several prominent Bank and FI boards across different countries.

S. Ram Kumar

S. Ram Kumar get bored easily. That explains the rest of this.

Ram studied electronics and then went on to do a PGDM at IIM, Ahmedabad. He then completed Masters in Nuclear Physics. 13 years of formal work included Multinations, Government, NGO, Section 25 and TRIPS stints. And then he quit to set up Last Resort, better known as www.luckfogic.com.

Ram has taught at around 25 B-Schools. He conducts corporate training programmes and takes consulting assignments of his interest. He does a lot of technical writing. And runs a magnificent woodworking studio-atelier out of Ahmedabad.

Ram Kumar play squash, is a serious angler. He loves unicycle, 4X4 and long distance motorcycling. He speaks eight languages and is currently learning 3 more. He cooks seriously and he takes pride in doing things as per his exacting standards and whatever else catches his attention and interests.

Sanjeev Kotnala

Sanjeev Kotnala has a rich experience of 32 years in Marketing and Brand Management. He invested his first 17 years in advertising with reputed leading agencies Mudra, HTA (JWT) and Lintas. Before founding INTRADIA WORLD (www.intradia.in) in 2014, he was Vice President National Marketing with Dainik Bhaskar Group, where he was part of core team to launch newspaper in Maharashtra, Punjab and Jharkhand and created many relevant and impactful properties for the brand.

Sanjeev is a Director in the South East Asia Board of 'Aid Et Action' an NGO. He is member Governing council of 'Indira Institute of Management Sudies'; Pune, adjunct Professor and senior advisor at MICA, Ahmedabad. He is also an ICF certified coach & NLP Practitioner.

Sanjeev conducts specialized workshops for corporate's. Some of his well-known workshops are, 'IdeaHARVEST', and 'InNoWait- no waiting for innovation'. He also conducts the unique workshop 'Brand-i- Be the brand'. He regularly blogs at www.sanjeevkotnala.com under the theme Perception Adulterated with Reality' and writes a weekly column KOTMARTIAL at www.mxmindia.com.

He is a voracious reader, a painter, storyteller and doodler. His published his debut novel 'CHIMERA OF LANSDOWNE' in 2018, and second book 'LIFE RELOADED – Real Life Real stories' in 2019. And this book 'REFLECTIONS' is his third book.

Satinder Pal Singh

Satinder Pal Singh is a Dairy technologist at heart. He is a Graduate from National Dairy research Institue, Karnal (Haryana) and a Post Graduate from IIM Ahmedabad. He is a professional with a proven track record and sound technical background with over 31 years of Industrial Experience with reputed MNCs.

Satinder is known for making a significant contribution in Product and Process Optimization while working with Nestle in India and International markets. He has repeatedly demonstrated capabilities and skill in building cost competitiveness, reduction of waste, removing inefficiencies from production systems, productivity improvement and enhancing team effectiveness.

Satinder has been a critical technical support pivot for markets like UK, US, Switzerland, Bulgaria, Ukraine, Turkey, Canada, Italy, Poland, Ecuador,Singapore and Malaysia. And has focussed on Technical Expertise in areas like Chocolate & Confectionery Manufacturing, Extrusion, Cocoa Processing, Dairy Technology, Milk and Milk Processing, Food Products Process Technology and Key Food Ingredients manufacturing processes, Wheat Flour – Milling. He holds a technical patent for Centre Filled Chocolate Manufacturing Process; granted by European Patent Office

Satinder is also a Faculty and assessor for TOT (NLRP)/ Support Training Partners for the training of Food Business Operators for FSSAI and FoSTaC- Food Safety and Training and Certification and prefers hands-on working with Business Partners.

S M Sundaram

Sundaram is Partner and CFO of Creaegis, an India focused private equity firm. His prior experiences of over 30 years include being CFO and Operating Partner at Baring Private Equity Partners India, CFO at CSS Corp, a San Jose based IT services company and stints at Sanmar Group and TVS Group in India. He has served on the boards of several companies in and outside India and is also a mentor and adviser to several early stage companies.

He is a Chartered Accountant, Cost Accountant, Company Secretary, Chartered Financial Analyst and a MBA from IIM Ahmedabad.

Sundaram is also an avid runner, having run several full and half marathons. He also volunteers with several non-profits. He can be contacted at reach.sundaram@gmail.com

Srikumar

Srikumar had a very successful 25+ years leadership career: spanning Country, Group and Global responsibilities across multinational banks, and regional organizations in the Banking and Payment Services space.

This, and successfully leading multi-ethnic teams across four continents, has stood him well in the current phase of career, where, for the last 3 years, he is Advisor to Boards on strategy, execution and risk mitigation. He can be contacted at hellosrikumar@gmail.com

Srinivas Shastrix

Srinivas Shastrix was born in Vizag in 1965, on the edge of infinity, with Ramakrishna Beach separating his house and the Bay of Bengal, the largest bay in the world

He studied Mechanical Engineering at Andhra University College of Engineering. He went to IIM, Ahmedabad, in the mid-1980s when he didn't know his @ss from his elbow and majored in Systems and Finance Work was a bit of a shock and somehow he did about 19 years of that, before retiring in 2006 for good. His best experience was working on the Executive Search app for Maars India, where he learned many nuggets about the Net such as async design

As per him, his real education started after He retired.

He can be contacted at shastrix@gmail.com

S Subramanian

For a person whose annual travel had been between Madras and Thrissoor till entering IIM Ahmedabad, he has worked across a spectrum of cities across the country. Finally he decided to pitch his tent in Delhi in circa 2000 - a city he saw for the first time in 1990 on a two day official trip.

He has always stuck to basic industries all along his corporate life, since his IIMA days. Gathering rust (steel industry), patients (emergency ambulance services), parcels (airport cargo terminal operation) and passengers (city bus service).

He bagged a B E (Mech) degree in from College of Engineering, Guindy. His school days were split between Kerala and Madras between Malayalam and English mediums. He worked as a service engineer for three years before joining IIMA.

He claims he has no specific hobbies and interests. What he likes is incessant chatting and he is known for his sharp observations.

Umesh Sharraf

Umesh Sharraf did his schooling at St Xavier's Bokaro; B.Tech. (Mechanical) from I.I.T. Kanpur in 1985; P.G.D.M. from I.I.M. Ahmedabad in 1987 & started his career in Bajaj Auto at Aurangabad. He joined the Indian Police Service in 1989. While in service, he completed L.L.B. from Kakatiya and S.K.Universities. He has worked as Asst. Superintendent of Police in Jagtial in Karimnagar District; as Addl. Superintendent of Police (Operations) Warangal and Karimnagar; as Superintendent of Police in Adilabad and Anantapur districts and in State Intelligence at Hyderabad and as Deputy Commissioner of Police (West Zone) in Hyderabad. As Dy. Inspector General of Police, he worked as DIG (Economic Offences) in CID at Hyderabad, as Commissioner of Police at Vijayawada and as Additional Director of the Anti Corruption Bureau at Hyderabad. As Inspector General of Police he worked as Addl. Director A.P. Police Academy, Jt. M.D. of AP TRANSCO, IG (E.O.W) and I.G. (Personnel) A.P. at Hyderabad. On promotion as ADG, he worked as Addl. D.G. (Personnel) of A.P. and after the bifurcation of the state, he held the charges of Personnel, Organisation and the Police Recruitment Board of Telangana.

He is the recipient of the National Vigilance Excellence Award in 2010 and 2011, United Nations Peace Medal in 1999, Internal Security Medal in 2004, Indian Police Medal for Meritorious Services in 2005, the President's Police Medal for Distinguished Services in 2014 and the FICCI SMART Policing Award in 2017. He joined the National Police Academy at Hyderabad as Joint Director in January 2015 and served there for 5 years

Acknowledgement

The list of people I would like to acknowledge for making this possible is long. However, I am going to highlight a few.

I would like to thank, my mother Mrs Kanchan Lata Kotnala and my in-laws Shri Ved Prakash Kundlia and Mrs Vijaya Kundlia. The sheer tingling of joy in their voice and pride in their eyes whenever a new book gets published makes me work more and more. Above all, thanks to my father Late Shri Ram Ballabh Kotnala who blesses us. I know, he would have been most happy with these developments.

Thanks to Neha my wife and my kids, Prateek and Preetica, who still wonder when and where do these books take shape. I will ask you to keep guessing. Thank you for giving me space and time to make this a possibility.

Thank you Neena Bagga, for blue-pencilling the manuscript. Ravi Bajpai, my ex-colleague from Dainik Bhaskar for the excellent cover design.

Thank you, my fellow contributing authors for being strong enough to publicly share a part of your life. I know, many limitations did not allow you to identify the place or people. I am happy to know all the stories are not only real-life stories but are something that had some impact on your life. This book could not have been possible without your help. Special thanks to A G Balasubramanian, Anchal Jan, Dinesh Gopalan, Dilip Thosar, Gyaneshway Tripathi, S Ram Kumar and S Subramanian. Thank you, for supporting the project.

Your confidence and suggestions helped a lot in making this book possible.

I have just one regret. We could not get any of the lady batch-mates to contribute. Hopefully, this book will find a sequel, and we will be able to rectify the mistake.

On the lighter side, I must thank WhatsApp. I can't think how this project could have been possible without it. Not only it eased sharing of concept, pushing the levers on group and individual basis, it was also the preferred mode of sharing updates and initial drafts.

Also, two free programmes to convert colour pictures into black and white images, namely 'ConvertImage' and 'Imgonline' have been of real help. Grammarly had been the basis first step check before Neena Bagga took the task to blue pencil the manuscript.

And finally, I thank Tarun at Penman Books, who has been quick in taking the project to its ultimate destination. They also published my second book 'Life Reloaded', and my experience with Penman Books has been excellent.

Manuscript Blue Pencilled by Neena Bagga

 Quietly powerful, strong, and individualistic, Neena Bagga speaking from a lifetime full of highs and lows, and with a quiet, warm spirituality that has made her a go-to role model and an Educator. Apart from being an avid narrator and an impulsive artist, she has dabbled in almost everything professionally from managing accounts to administration to being the director of a company herself.

Having devoted herself to being a mother, a wife, and a humanitarian; Neena has now set off to continue her legacy of 20 years of educating and helping parents and students by conducting seminars and workshops through Education Personified Coaching Classes.

In addition to all this and more, She is an editor par excellence.

Neena is often found saying, "Don't let mental blocks control you. Set yourself free. Confront your fear and turn the mental blocks into building blocks."

Cover Design by Ravi Bajpai

Ravi Bjapai is a highly creative and multitalented Graphic Designer with extensive experience of close to 18 years across multimedia, marketing and print design. He has exceptional collaborative and interpersonal skills. A dynamic team player with well-developed written and verbal communication abilities. Additionally Ravi is highly skilled in client and vendor relations. Talented at building and maintaining "win-win" partnerships. Accustomed to performing in deadline-driven environments with an emphasis on working within budget requirements.

Books by Class of '87, IIMA

FPM joining IIMA in 1985 shared their first year classes with the PGP-1985-87. The batch considers them member 'Class of 1987'.

ANKUR MITTAL
What Happens in Office Stays in Office

An account of life in the cut-throat world of large corporations, told in a unique humorous and ironical style through short stories. The domineering boss, the whining employee, the counter-productive policy-making, the jockeying for visibility, are all products of this interesting world. In the garb of humour and satire, this book delivers some hard-hitting management lessons and lets out some secrets of success of the corporate world.

ANKUR MITTAL
Some Methods Some Madness

In a dynamic business world, the world of BPO business is perhaps even more dynamic. This comprehensive edition aims to capture the essence of managing the diverse and ever-changing domain of the BPO business and the day to day challenges and possibilities that are faced and offered by the industry. Having an industry perspective, this book serves as a convenient guide for

all those individuals who are involved with the BPO industry in one way or the other and also for those who aspire to carve a career in the realm of BPOs.

ASHOK PANJWANI (Co-Author)
Financing and Managing Projects- Volume I and II

Project is an instrument of change and no project is complete unless its objective is achieved. Every project is specific and unique and the term ÒprojectÓ is constantly expanding and ever changing. This first volume deals with the managerial aspects of a project, i.e., project phases; its formulation and appraisal techniques; there is no single best technique and executive judgment is essential. Every chapter outlines the objectives to be delivered and includes project instances, brief case examples, and case studies that provide an analytical kit for executives and professionals. The book makes for a lucid reading and serves as a guide for the reader. It has been written based on our experiences

gained and feedback collected from teaching, training, and delivering various consultancy projects..

GANESH PRASAD
Dependence-Oriented Thinking.

Service-Oriented Architecture (SOA) is a somewhat disappointing technology buzzword from the last decade, associated with expensive and heavyweight technology that does not provide as much of a return on investment as was hyped - or is it? Has the industry just failed to understand and exploit the power of SOA?

Ganesh Prasad, an industry veteran has discovered the secret to unlocking SOA's wasted potential. He aims to reignite SOA practice with a fresh, lightweight yet rigorous method based on the single most important element that underlies all types of system interactions - the notion of dependencies. "Dependency-Oriented Thinking" is the book that reveals these secrets for the first time.

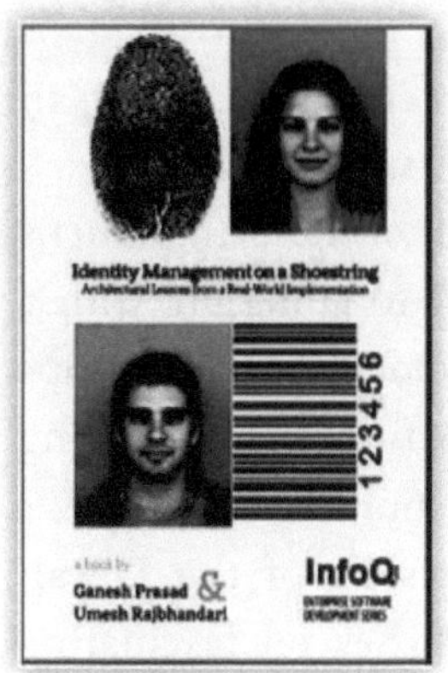

GANESH PRASAD
Beginning PHP4

This book is a complete tutorial in PHP's language features and functionality, beginning with the basics and building up to the design and construction of complex data-driven websites. Fully working examples in the book include a directory-style web search engine, a mailing list management system, a web-based file editor, and a graphical online shopping mall guidebook.

Anybody who knows HTML can use this book. If you've done any programming, that will be useful, but it's not a requirement. You can run all of the code on either a Windows or UNIX (e.g., Linux) system, and the book explains how to set up a web server and database in both of these environments

GANESH PRASAD (co-author)
Identity management on a Shoe String

This book is aimed at Security and IT practitioners (especially architects) in end-user organisations who are responsible for implementing an enterprise-wide Identity and Access Management (IAM) system. It is neither a conceptual treatment of Identity nor a detailed technical manual on a particular product. It describes a pragmatic and cost-effective architectural approach to implementing IAM within an organisation, based on the experience of the authors.

HARISH BHAT

The Curious Marketer: Expeditions in Branding and Consumer Behaviour

From brand marketing using aliens and flying saucers to going big with a delicious local product (banana chips or coconut water), from the interesting concept behind multicoloured socks to the metamorphosis of the Diwali shopper, Bhat touches on fascinating areas that marketers are targeting today.Immensely topical, this is a pleasurable read that will be of great interest to general readers, as well as students and professionals who work in the exciting area of marketing.

HARISH BHAT

Tatalog: Eight Modern Stories from a Timeless Institution

TATA, is a name recognised by almost every Indian. Tatalog: Eight Modern Stories from A Timeless Institution provides readers with an insider glimpse of the challenges faced by the TATA companies and how they rose above it all and carved a name for themselves. The book vividly brings forth never-before-heard-of, actual cases faced by TATA companies, which have a strong presence in steel, automobiles, IT, beverages and groceries to name a few.

HARISH BHAT
An Extreme Love of Coffee (Novel)

When they drink a cup of 'magic' coffee, Rahul and Neha are entrusted with a quest that promises to lead to great treasure. As they race from the plantations of Coorg to Japanese graveyards, they are trailed by the Yamamoto brothers-bearing grudges and carrying swords. Accompanied by a friendly ghost and armed with an extreme love of coffee, Rahul and Neha discover their passion for warm frothy concoctions and each other.

But will they manage to evade their Japanese assailants and find the treasure they first set out for?

JANAT SHAH
Supply Chain Management. Text and Cases

Supply Chain Management: Text and Cases integrates concepts and application to turn the spotlight on innovations-the need of the hour in supply chain management. Janat adopts a reader-friendly approach to introduce the fundamentals to both students and practitioners. This five part book presents numerous examples and caselets, thus blending concepts with current industrial practices and state-of-the-art know-how, for enhanced understanding and a holistic view of supply chain management.

JANAT SHAH
Operational Research in Indian Steel industry
The book contains the papers presented at the Workshop oh Operational Research in Steel Industry, organized at the Bhilai Steel Plant of Steel Authority of India Ltd., during March 5-6, 1990 in an edited form. The workshop was organised by Operational Research Society of India and was sponsored by Steel Authority of India Ltd. and the Tata Iron and Steel Company Ltd.

MOHYNA SRINIVASAN
The House On Mall Road
In The House on Mall Road Mohyna Srinivasan gives us a unique glimpse of life in the army-the hospitality of the people, their kindness and affection, the quaint yet charming traditions that uphold authority and valour while always maintaining respect and camaraderie. Dramatic and riveting, The House on Mall Road is a spellbinding debut novel.

RAGHURAM G RAJAN
Saving Capatalism from the Capatalists

For nearly two centuries, scholars and politicians have debated the future of capitalism. Raghuram G. Rajan, and co-author Luigi Zingales, argue that free, healthy and competitive financial markets occupy this very delicate middle ground. They are an extraordinarily effective tool in spreading opportunity and fighting poverty. Without them, economies would invariably ossify and decline. Yet, financial markets are among the most highly criticized and least understood parts of the capitalist system-because of the executives who extol their virtues with every breath while attempting to extinguish them with every action.

RAGHURAM G RAJAN
Fault Lines

In Fault Lines, Rajan demonstrates how unequal access to education and health care in the United States puts us all in deeper financial peril, even as the economic choices of countries like Germany, Japan, and China place an undue burden on America to get its policies right. He outlines the hard choices we need to make to ensure a more stable world economy and restore lasting prosperity.

RAGHURAM G RAJAN
I Do What I do

I Do What I Do offers a front-row view into the thinking of one of the world's most respected economists, one whose commitment to India's progress shines through in the essays and speeches here. It also brings home what every RBI Governor discovers for himself when he sits down at his desk on the 18th floor: the rupee stops here. Right here!

RAGHURAM G RAJAN
The Third Pillar

Economists all too often understand their field as the relationship between markets and the state, and they leave squishy social issues for other people. That's not just myopic, Rajan argues; it's dangerous. All economics is actually socioeconomics - all markets are embedded in a web of human relations, values and norms. Rajan presents a way to rethink the relationship between the market and civil society and argues for a return to strengthening and empowering local communities as an antidote to growing despair and unrest.

The Third Pillar is a masterpiece of explication, a book that will be a classic for its offering of a wise, authoritative and humane explanation of the forces that have wrought such a sea change in our lives.

RADHIKA CHADHA
Basava And The Dots Of Fire
Every day, Basava goes to the forest to collect firewood for his mother. But one day it grows dark and he can't find his way home. That is when Basava sees the glowing dots of fire that light up the forest... A gentle story with a touch of magic and dramatic illustrations.

RADHIKA CHADHA
I Am So Sleepy
Bahadur, the little elephant has forgotten how to sleep. Worried, and very, very sleepy he goes to his animal friends for help. But they all sleep in their own different ways — elephants don't sleep like that! What should Bahadur do? A charming story with pictures that give each animal a special, lovable character.

RADHIKA CHADHA
Snoring Shanmugam
The animals from the popular I'm So Sleepy are back! Shanmugam the lion is supposed to be the king of the jungle but all he does is sleep. Worse, he snores. Then one day, another lion enters the jungle. He is lean and mean — he is Gabbar Singh. The other animals are frightened, but how can they get the lazy Shanmugam to awake to their defence? Bahadur the little elephant has a brilliant idea . . .

RADHIKA CHADHA
Colour – Colour- Kamini

Kapila Aunty is teaching the little chameleons how to change colour, one at a time. But Kamini gets excited and goes red, purple, green, yellow . . .she can't stop! Meet baby elephant Bahadur's new friend in the third book in the series.

RADHIKA CHADHA
Malipoo, Where Are You?

When Paytu the pig goes on a sugarcane walk with Amma the elephant and Hutoxi the horse, she asks Anna and Akka to look after her babies. But the two elephant teenagers get busy in a game of coconut-football... and the piglets disappear! Another story in the popular series about little Bahadur and his animal friends.

RADHIKA CHADHA
Yes, Hutoxi!

Mannu, Chandu, Anna and Akka are fed up of Hutoxi the horse – she snorts and scolds and spoils their fun. And then suddenly one day, Hutoxi disappears. Where has she gone? Will she never come back? Baby Bahadur and his animal friends return in this fifth book of the endearing series.

KUMAR SANAL VELYADHUN
Rural Marketing: Targeting the Non-urban Consumer

This highly practical and informative book provides unique insights into the essential features of rural markets in India as well as challenges posed by the rural consumer. Retaining the managerial perspective of the first edition, this second edition has been thoroughly revised and expanded, and examines in greater detail the concept of rural markets and rural marketing. It also contains numerous short cases to illustrate how social and cultural habits influence rural consumer behaviour.

KUMAR SANAL VELYADHUN
Marketing to Rural Consumers: Understanding and Tapping the Rural Market Potential

The book covers 28 selected and edited papers presented at the 'Marketing to Rural Consumers - Understanding and Tapping the Marketing Potential' conference. This book contains in the conference. These papers are presented in six sections: Boundaries of Rural Market; Environment of the Rural Consumer: Agriculture, Development Issues and ICTs; The Rural Consumer; Factors influencing the Rural Consumer Behavior; Communication and Channels in Rural Markets; and, The Rural Consumer and Implications for Marketing Strategy.

KUMAR SANAL VELYADHUN
Rural Marketing

Result of the 2nd conference on marketing to rural consumers held in 2009. The book covers select papers from the conference

SANJEEV KOTNALA

Chimera of Lansdowne (Fiction)

The lives of five residents of the sleepy little town of Lansdowne in Uttarakhand is loosely connected. They have all been at the receiving end of independent unexplained experiences. Their past is intertwined with their present and maybe the future, in case it exists.

They can only succeed collectively by joining forces. However, success is one of the many possibilities. They don't know the unseen. They have no idea what the Chimera of Lansdowne is. They must explore the only direction they have.

Will they come together to take advantage of a once in a lifetime alignment of celestial bodies? Time like always is limited. Will they be able to connect all the dots and find the key? Will they succeed in breaking the cycle?

SANJEEV KOTNALA

Life Reaload. Real Life . RealStories

Life Reloaded, is an unique Anthology of Real Life, Real People, Real Stories. Life is like an overwhelming TV serial where episodes start every moment. One can't change the events, sequences, characters, emotions, actions and outcomes of the past episodes. However, one can Pause, Reflect, Absorb the learnings. And then Move on without the past baggage. Based on past experiences and learning, one can control the narrative and flow of the new chapters in life.

In 'Life Reloaded', fourteen professionals share stroies from their professional and personal life. Incidents that in some way impacted the contributing author's life. What you take out from them is up to you. Reading these experiences, you too would want to Pause, Reflect, Absorb and Move On. Dig into life's impact incidents. Reflect on the situations. Maybe you will encounter some hidden learnings. You owe it to yourself!

SUMAN SRIVASTAVA

Marketing Unplugged

Marketing Unplugged is a toolkit of new techniques that you should use to come up with your marketing strategy. This book speaks of experts who tell us that it is better to observe behaviour than to ask questions in research. This startlingly simple credo has been forgotten in the excitement of projective techniques and ever more sophisticated data analysis.

There are several other ideas that experts have come up with. This book is a combination of some of those ideas into a new narrative titled 'Marketing Unplugged'.

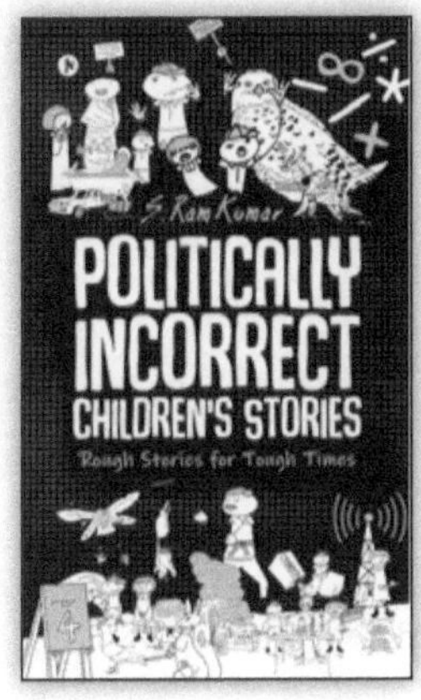

S RAM KUMAR

'Politically Incorrect Children's Stories'. Industrial-strength stories treat children and adults as equals. And told it as it is. No pussy-footing, moral science or sugar coating. Spades are spades! No quarter given, none taken. No mythical characters beggaring belief and science. Just brute logic and empirical evidence. Two kids, Bila & Kabun; a dog - Mr. Morkley and a story-mongering PICS Dad explore the world around them. Meant to be bedtime stories, they mostly left the teller and the listeners sleepless.

SRINIVAS SHASTRI

'Brushes with Brahmn ~ Dancing with my Datta'

From having a super-duper education to a so-so career, the author retired at the age of 41 to have quite some time to Rumi-nate, with valuable inputs from his Datta of Shirdi Baba, Sri Ramakrishna, and Sri Ramana Maharshi

He found that he didn't exist separate from the world but was very much a part of it and, more importantly, he didn't have to change the world, it was enough if he changed himself and the world would change to that extent…

Class of '87, IIMA

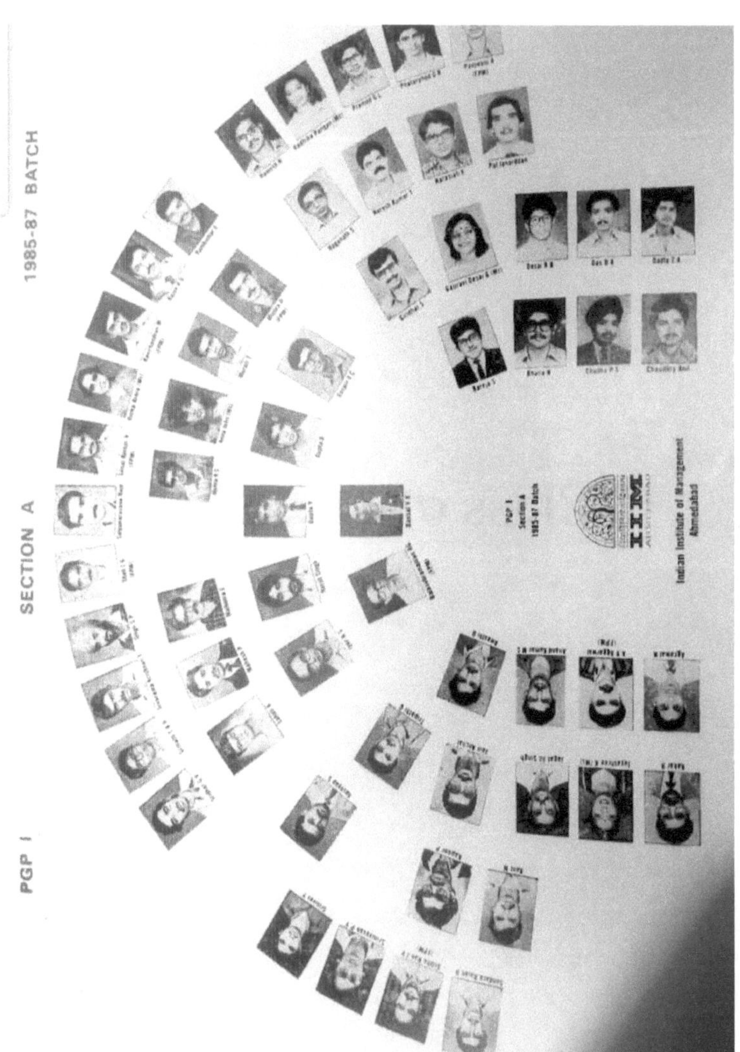

ALPHABETICAL LIST BATCH 1985-87 IIMA

1. A K Aggarwal FPM
2. Ajit Bhushan
3. Ajwani Rajesh
4. Anand Kumar M C
5. Anna John
6. Annu Ratta
7. Ashish Kumar
8. Asthana Roopam
9. Awasthi Rajul
10. Awasthi Rajul
11. Balasubramanian A G FPM
12. Bansal Vijay K
13. Bareja Sanjay
14. Bhandari Karan S
15. Bhat Harish R
16. Bhatia Nipun
17. Bhatia Rajat
18. Bhatia Rakesh
19. Bioin Bihari
20. Bobde Sanjay
21. Brijesh Kapil
22. Chadha Parminder S
23. Chandra Shekhar K
24. Chaudhary Amitabh
25. Chaudhary Anil
26. Dadla Zaheer A
27. Daruvala M N
28. Das Debutosh K
29. Dasgupta S
30. Deb Asesh K
31. Deo Ashish K
32. Desai Gauravi
33. Desai Rantim B
34. Dey Bashob
35. Dey Sanjoy
36. Dharmender Kumar
37. Dinesh Gopalan
38. Dharmender Kumar
39. Dinesh Gopalan
40. Duryodhan S G
41. Giridhar S
42. Gokale S
43. Gosain Varun C
44. Govind Menon
45. Gupta Avinash
46. Gupta Vivek
47. Gurnani D
48. Hari R
49. Harinath K B
50. Harjit Singh
51. Hina Sachdeva
52. Iyer Anil S
53. Jagatjit Singh
54. Jain Anchal
55. Jain Harshit H
56. Jain Rajat K
57. Jangeed R L
58. Jasmeet Kaur
59. Jaya Sharma
60. Jayashree K
61. Johri Nikhil

62. Kakkar Rajeev
63. Kant Mani
64. Kapoor Kapil
65. Kapoor Nalin B
66. Kapoor Pankaj
67. Kapur Ajay S
68. Kashyap Sudhir
69. Kerketta Praveen K
70. Kohli Chiranjeev
71. Krishna T
72. Kumar E
73. Kumar Ramanathan
74. Lahoti Alok
75. Lal Rajiv
76. Malhotra Sumit
77. Malik Tarun
78. Manikkam N
79. Manoj Kumar
80. Meenakshi Nath
81. Mehta A G
82. Menon Raja
83. Menon Vinod P
84. Merja Hasmukh
85. Milind Kulkarni
86. Mishra Debi FPM
87. Mishra Shreejit
88. Mithal Ankur
89. Mitra Atish
90. Mohyna Khurana
91. Mondal Tejmoy
92. Mukherjee Monojit
93. Murali Thadi
94. Nachiket Mor
95. Nadarajan V C
96. Nagamani U
97. Naganath S
98. Nageswara Rao G V
99. Naik Lalit
100. Namrata Kaul
101. Nanda Sandeep K
102. Narasiah Venkatesh
103. Pal Janardhan
104. Pal Sandeep
105. Panjwani Ashok FPM
106. Paul Debkanti
107. Phaneesh M
108. Phatarpod Girish R
109. Pramod G L
110. Prasad G C
111. Radhika Puri
112. Radhika Rangan
113. Rajan R G
114. Ram Mohan N
115. Ramachandran Raghu
116. Ramakrishna D
117. Ramaswami Seshan
118. Ramesh D
119. Ramesh N
120. Ramkumar S
121. Ratnaleela B
122. Ravi Shankar S
123. Ravichandran D
124. Ravichandran M FPM
125. Ravindran N

126. Richa Arora
127. Roy A
128. Sanal Kumar V FPM
129. Sanjeev Kotnala
130. Sankar G
131. Sashi R
132. Sastry. S.V.N
133. Satyanarayana Raju
134. Seetharaman L
135. Sehgal Ajay
136. Sehgal Vivek
137. Shah Apoorva L
138. Shah Janat G FPM
139. Shahra Umesh
140. ShanmughasundaramN
141. Sharraf Umesh
142. Shekhar Vidhu
143. Shishir Mohan Kumar
144. Shormila Gupta (Ms)
145. Singh S P
146. Sirish C V
147. Sivarama Krishnan T
148. SivaramasubramanianR
149. Soans Fred
150. Sreeram T
151. Sridhar G V
152. Srikumar M Raman
153. Srinath T A P
154. Srinivas P S
155. Srinivas Y
156. Srinivasan Ajay
157. Srinivasan N
158. Srinivasan Prasanna V
159. Srinvas V
160. Srivastava
161. Srivastava S
162. Subramanian N
163. Subramanian S
164. Sundara Rajan H
165. Sundara Rajan R (Late)
166. Sundaram S M
167. Sundaresan N
168. Sunderarajan G S
169. Thosar Dilip
170. Tripathi Gyaneshwar
171. Uthayakumar T R
172. Vadivel T
173. Varghese Sunil S
174. Venaik Sunil
175. Venkat Venkat
176. Venkatesan A
177. Venkatesh A S
178. Venugopal C J
179. Vinay Kumar Mahajan
180. Vinita V K

This is the sample call letter that the batch was sent on April 27, 1985

INDIAN INSTITUTE OF MANAGEMENT

Vastrapur, Ahmedabad 380 015

Gram : INDINMAN   Telex : 121-351 IIMA IN   Phone : 407241

Ref. No.   05460/   1985-87

April 27. 1985

Mr S M Sundaram
70/2 MIG Flats, First Avenue
Ashok Nagar
MADRAS 600 083

Mr S M Sundaram
S/O Sri G Sivarama Krishnan
Sr.Secd. Supervisor, Office of the D.E,
Telegraphs, Mettupalayam Road,
COIMBATORE 641 043

Dear Mr Sundaram:

I am glad to inform you that you have been selected for provisional admission to IIMA's Post-Graduate Programme in Management for the session beginning July 2. 1985. subject to your fulfilling the following conditions :

1. Your written acceptance of this admission offer with acceptance fee of Rs. 500 (demand draft in favour of "Indian Institute of Management, Ahmedabad") must reach me latest by Saturday, May 25, 1985. Please use Annexure IV for accepting the admission offer. The acceptance fee is NOT refundable if you do not join the Programme. But it will be adjusted towards your caution deposit at the time of registration if you join the Programme.

2. You must personally report for registration at the Institute on Tuesday, July 2. 1985, at 10.00 a.m. and

   a) Submit attested true copies of all marksheets and the originals on the registration day and satisfy that there is no discrepancy in the information given in the application, photo copies, and originals.

   b) If you are appearing for the final year bachelor's examination, you must produce evidence of having passed the Bachelor's degree with minimum 50% aggregate marks (45% for SC/ST) from the appropriate University/Institute Authority.

   c) If you belong to Scheduled Caste/Tribe. you must submit the original SC/ST certificate along with an attested true copy.

THIS ADMISSION OFFER WILL AUTOMATICALLY STAND CANCELLED IF YOU FAIL TO COMPLY WITH ANY CONDITIONS MENTIONED ABOVE, AND THE DECISION OF THE INSTITUTE IN THIS REGARD WILL BE FINAL.

3. If you have applied for the Specialization Programme in Agriculture, you will not be permitted to change to the general stream and vice versa.

4. If you have applied as a Scheduled Caste/Tribe candidate and it is found at any time that you are not a bonafide Scheduled Caste/Tribe candidate, this offer of admission will be automatically cancelled and you will be expelled from the Institute if you are already admitted to the Programme.

5. For other information, please see the enclosed folder "Information for Students."

Looking forward to hearing from you soon and with best wishes.

Yours sincerely,

R.P.S. Yadav
Admission Officer

And this was the welcome letter sent in May 1985

INDIAN INSTITUTE OF MANAGEMENT STUDENTS' ASSOCIATION
Vastrapur, Ahmedabad-380 015

Gram: INDINMAN   Telex: 12-351 IIMA IN   Phone: 450041

May 27, 1985

Dear .S.V............,

Congratulations and welcome to the beautiful world of IIM-'A'.
We, the second year students of PGP and senior FPMs, are looking
forward to having you here with us shortly.

The purpose of this letter is to give you some inside info about
this place. Around this time last year, we were wondering what
IIMA was all about. One - year stay here has provided us with
much information which we would like to share with you.

The specially architectured IIMA campus is situated in a serene
locale, on the outskirts of the city of Ahmedabad. The campus
houses roughly 400 students and 100 faculty members. Facilities
on the campus include a :

* STUDENTS STORES (SS) - (Where you can help yourself
                to anything from stationery items to slippers
                to T-Shirts to buckets).

* ICE CREAM PARLOUR (ICP) - for one with a sweet tooth -
                you can choose from among half doz to a doz
                varieties.

* MUSIC ROOM - For the musically inclined, we have a
                full-fledged music-room complete with a
                stereo system and plenty of records.

* SBI BRANCH   * POST OFFICE   * DISPENSARY

* Good facilities exist for sports. We also have a well
  equipped Gym and Photography Club.

The IIMA students Association is called " STUDENTS AFFAIRS
COUNCIL" - 'SAC' for short. SAC organises all the extra
curricular activities which form an integral part of our life
here. These include literary, music, sports and a variety of
other activities. We suggest that you bring along with you,
your musical instruments, sports gear and of coz, "loads of
talents".

...2

: 2 :

About the climate here, Aug and Sept are quite wet while Dec and Jan get pretty chilly (5°c). You needn't get your winter-wear rightaway, 'coz you get a 12-day break after your first term (some time at the end of Sept). Also don't burden yourself with buckets, cloth-hangers, stationery etc. as the Students Stores is well equipped to cater to your needs.

Ah yes ! We almost forgot all about academics. As can be expected in a professional institution like IIMA, academics do take a major chunk of your time. The 3-storeyed Vikram Sarabhai Library is the ideal refuge for the highly studious species. More about academics when you get here in person.

<u>Now, About Your Arrival Here:-</u>

The railway station is 9 Kms from here and the airport is roughly 15 Kms away. Autorikshaws are the main mode of transport and the charges would be around Rs.13/- and Rs.25/- respectively. Ask for "Management, Vastrapur, near Atira".

If you are coming by one of the following trains we'll be there at the station to meet you.

Train No. & Name	From	Arrival Time	On
1 Dn Gujarat Mail	Bombay	6.30a.m.	30/6, 1/7&2/7
505 Up Ashram Express	Delhi	10.40a.m.	30/6
134 Up Howrah-A'bad Express	Calcutta	3.00p.m.	29/6 & 30/6
166 Up Sabarmati Express	Faizabad/ Lucknow	7.10a.m.	1/7 & 2/7
146 Up Navjivan Express	Madras	8.30p.m.	28/6

Do fill in the attached sheet and let us know at the earliest about your arrival.

In case you would want to have any clarifications/information, please do write to Mr. N V Pillai, SAC Office, IIM, Ahmedabad 380 015.

We are sure you are itching to come down to this place (after reading this letter). We, on our part, would be happy to have you amongst us and are awaiting your arrival. Come, bring your cheerfulself along to IIM-"A" - A UNIQUE EXPERIENCE YOU WOULD NEVER FORGET.

M.A. RAVI KUMAR
CO-ORDINATOR
STUDENTS AFFAIRS COUNCIL
(IIMA STUDENTS ASSOCIATION)

P.S. :-   GET SOME EATS
          PREFERABLY SWEETS.

OoooOoooO

The Annexure Of The Call Letter Detailing The Fee That The Class Of 1987 Had To Pay In First Year

ANNEXURE I

PAYMENT SCHEDULE

Acceptance Fee (Due on May 25, 1985)
Fee (non-refundable) payable by
the first year students at the time
of acceptance of admission offer — Rs. 500*

YEARLY EXPENSES

Caution Deposit	Rs. 500*
Tuition	500
Computer	400
Room and Electricity	630
Students Welfare Activity	160
Books and Teaching Materials	900**
Mess (9 months — vegetarian)	2,700**
(9 months — non-vegetarian)	3,300**

These estimates do not include expenses on travel, clothing, laundry, and other personal items.

First Term (Due on July 2, 1985)

1.	Tuition	Rs. 200
2.	Computer	100
3.	Mess Deposit	300***
4.	Room Rent & Electricity	210
5.	Books and Teaching Materials	300
6.	Students Welfare Activity	160
7.	Students Store	35
	Total amount payable on the registration day	Rs. 1,305

Second Term (Due on October 7, 1985)

1.	Tuition	Rs. 200
2.	Computer	150
3.	Room Rent & Electricity	210
4.	Books and Teaching Materials	300
5.	Mess Deposit	150
		Rs. 1,010

Third Term (Due on January 15, 1985)

1.	Tuition	Rs. 100
2.	Computer	150
3.	Room Rent & Electricity	210
4.	Books and Teaching Materials	300
5.	Mess Deposit	150
		Rs. 910

* Will be treated as caution deposit, and it is refundable on satisfactory completion of the Programme.

** Estimated expenses to be charged on actuals.

*** Will be adjusted against mess dues for March/April 1986.

www.ingramcontent.com/pod-product-compliance
Lightning Source LLC
Chambersburg PA
CBHW061430150726
47987CB00001B/158